"*No Sex in the City* is a must-read for single w⟨ ⟩ refreshing honesty and humor with a despera⟨ ⟩ equip and encourage you in your pursuit of godliness and sexual purity. Read this book individually, with your girlfriends, or with your book club."

—Gwen Smith
Author of *Broken into Beautiful*
Cofounder of Girlfriends in God

"*No Sex in the City* is real, edgy, and offers in-your-face biblical truth about a topic we all need to hear the truth about. Everyone who is dating needs to read this book and take its message to heart."

—Miles McPherson
Pastor, The Rock Church, San Diego, CA

"Lindsey Isham candidly shares her struggles with purity in a way that Christians think about, but don't always communicate openly. Her writing style is both hilarious and deeply challenging. *No Sex in the City* is powerful, significant, and critical in helping young women live a virtuous life, regardless of their past."

—Bill McCartney
Former University of Colorado head football coach
Founder and CEO, Promise Keepers

"This disarmingly honest book will engage you, not only because of the topic, but because of the often humorous way Lindsey Isham weaves in stories. Readers will find this book challenging and encouraging to their faith because of Lindsey's passionate faith in the Lord—the way she trusts Him to be faithful and chooses daily to obey Him in the area of sexual purity."

—Gayle B. Parker
President, Compelling Communication

NO SEX IN THE CITY

One Virgin's Confessions on Love, Lust, Dating, and Waiting

Lindsey N. Isham

Kregel
Publications

No Sex in the City: One Virgin's Confessions on Love, Lust, Dating, and Waiting

© 2009 by Lindsey N. Isham

Published by Kregel Publications, a division of Kregel, Inc., P.O. Box 2607, Grand Rapids, MI 49501.

Library of Congress Cataloging-in-Publication Data
Isham, Lindsey N.
   No sex in the city : one virgin's confessions on love, lust, dating, and waiting / Lindsey N. Isham.
     p. cm.
   Includes bibliographical references and index.
   1. Sexual abstinence—Religious aspects—Christianity. 2. Christian women—Sexual behavior. 3. Single people—Sexual behavior. I. Title.
BT708.I84   2009   241'.66082—dc22   2009008238

ISBN 978-0-8254-2906-4

Printed in the United States of America

09 10 11 12 13 / 5 4 3 2 1

To every young woman
who needs to hear someone say,
"You are worth waiting for."

Contents

Acknowledgments

THANK YOU GOD FOR PROTECTING ME and blessing me with a heart for purity; I could not be the woman I am today without You. Thank You for never giving up on me, even when I disappointed You with my thoughts and actions.

Thank you Mom, Meech, and Jaden. Because of your love, I am convinced that we have the best family ever! You three inspire me in ways that words cannot convey. Thank you Dad for all of your encouragement and support with this book. I love you guys.

Thank you to my deceased stepdad, Mark, and the parents who raised him. He was a godly man who stood for integrity, love, and wisdom. His life reminded our family of how intimately God really loves us. Someday, I hope to marry a man like him.

Thank you to all of my immediate and extended family. I love you guys.

Thank you Judith, my mentor, for lovingly guiding me toward Jesus and helping shape the woman I am today.

Thank you Stacey Johnson, my roommate, for your support and for letting me transform our place into a coffeehouse. You are such a blessing to me!

Thank you Nick Turrieta, aka the Webmaster, for all the computer help. I couldn't have set up my Web site without you!

Thank you Peter Carney (http://peterjcarney.com) for the great photo on the back cover.

Thank you to all the people who encouraged me to pursue my

dream of being a published author. Thank you to all my friends and accountability partners who lovingly kept me in check all these years. Thank you to my guy friends who have loved me like a sister and have been an example of what a godly man looks like. Thank you to each of you who prayed faithfully for me, this book, and its readers.

Growing up I had so many family friends whose marriages inspired me and gave me hope for the future. Thank you to Ron and Eleanor Barley, Gene and Andrea Binder, Stuart and Manon Crespi, Jack and Sue Howard, Eddie and Cindi Listander, Tom and Gayle Parker, Gene and Judith Schneider, Terry and Denise Simmons, Mark and Karen Stevens, and Gino and Laura Ward.

Thank you to all of my married friends who are faithful and committed to each other; you bless me.

Thank you to my agent, Bill Jensen. You are such an encourager; thank you for all your hard work.

Thank you to Kregel Publications for partnering with me.

And finally, thank you to those of you who helped me edit this book: Mom (seriously, you are the best), Rabbi Gene Binder, Pastor Steve and Linda Brown, Andrea Garcia, Kristen Johnson, Stacey Johnson, Melissa Kirkham, Rachel Kumar, Christopher McShane, Gracie Mentry, Carolyn Mott, Erika Payne, Dave Plati, Carolyn Rossi, Judith Schneider, and the staff at Kregel.

CHAPTER 1

You're a What?

I AM A THIRTY-YEAR-OLD VIRGIN on purpose, not by accident, and I am *so* horny. Yes, that's right, I want sex! In fact, I am sure that I need it. *Am I allowed to say that? Am I wrong for thinking that?* For some reason I love talking about sex (or should I say the lack thereof?). I heard rumors that the average American woman marries by age twenty-four, but when I researched it further, I found out that statistic was true in the 1970s.[1] Today the average age is about twenty-six.[2] How the heck did I get to be thirty and still unmarried? It sounds surreal when I actually say it out loud: "I am a thirty-year-old virgin." I don't think I'm old, but for some reason I thought I would have had sex by now.

I was twenty, a sophomore in college, when I first heard a man teach a biblical view of sex. *The Bible talks about sex?* I had no idea. So, for the past ten years, I've been excited about sex. I'll open books and turn straight to what I call the "good chapters." Why not skim those chapters first? If you are anything like me, you probably looked at the table of contents in this book and skipped straight to chapter 10—the *sex* chapter. If you did, welcome back to the beginning. The way I see it, it never hurts to reread the sex chapter, right?

I don't consider myself a violent individual, but sometimes I feel like shooting the person who said that women don't reach their sexual peak until age thirty-five. Here's the thing: If I am not in my sexual peak right now, then what the heck is happening to me? Some people have said, "It's just stress." Others have said, "It's just because you are a virgin." *Hmm.* Recently I confessed to my mentor, Judith, that I am constantly thinking about sex. She just smiled and said this was normal. Normal! I rarely hear other single, Christian women talking about how horny they are. Only guys are supposed to have this problem, right? If I have six more years of singleness with the constant onslaught of sexual thoughts and desires, I just might go postal.

I guess I am in what you could call a "pre-postal" stage in my life. I have been in this stage for at least eight years, and I don't know how much longer I can take it. Because I have been deprived of sex for far too long, I sometimes feel that at any minute I could be the front-page story that reads, "Virgin Girl Goes Postal." I suppose I could move to the mountains and live like a Lumber Jill—alone, with a dog, and far away from gorgeous men, sexualized media, and everything else that makes me think about sex. Maybe then my sexual desires would ease up a bit. In the meantime, I live in a city, have a regular job, and am trying to stop the progression of my "pre-postal" condition. So far I have seen very little progress.

I am surrounded by awkward men who think that virgins are fictional characters in Greek myths. This must explain why they are so shocked when they find out that I am still a virgin. If only I could come up with a way to give guys advanced notice about my virginity. You see, I figure that if men are forewarned, we can spend the majority of the conversation centered on something other than my sexual choices. Not that my sexual choices aren't important, valuable, or interesting, because they are. It is just *really* difficult to get to know a guy when he is stuttering, "So you speak about abstinence for a living? You actually believe that people can get married without ever having sex? Oh, you are proof that it's possible to be abstinent. So, uh . . . um, you're a—so you have never, uh . . . How do I say this?"

I reply with a smile and say, "It's okay. You can say it. Yes, I am a virgin."

"You're a what?"

When a guy finds out that I am a virgin, in between stumbling over his words, he looks at me as if I were an alien. You know the look: blank stare, jaw wide open, crinkled forehead. It's as if I have a third eye or eight arms. Then, once he processes the whole "virgin thing," he hesitates because he is looking for a politically correct way to identify me. For some reason, the term *virgin* is not politically correct anymore. In fact, in a recent survey, 26 percent of teens said, "It's embarrassing to admit being a virgin."[3] Maybe I should call myself a more socially acceptable term, something other than virgin. I just looked up "virgin" in the dictionary. How about *unadulterated* or *immaculate*?

"You're Going to Get Laid"

I am not an alien, I am a virgin! Some people think they are one and the same, which was why I was the girl that the boys made the bets about. I will never forget the day in high school when this scrawny, arrogant, and quite stupid freshman boy approached me in the lunch room. He informed me that I was the center of a bet and he was the lucky guy who would win. Before I had a chance to tell him that I wasn't interested in whatever he was about to say, he smiled and said, "We made a bet to see who would be the first guy to get you laid." *What an idiot.* Why do guys make these bets? Do they think that it makes them more manly?

After he said this I leaned forward and put my hand on his shoulder. I moved in close to whisper something in his ear. After all, his buddies were watching from across the cafeteria and I had to make it juicy. I took him by surprise with one swift knee to his groin. *Yes! She shoots, she scores! That's what you get, you jerk!* I took pleasure in watching him crouch to the ground, face scrunched, hands trying to ease the pain. After checking to make sure I didn't break a nail or something awful like that, I towered over him and said, "You are talking to the wrong girl because *that* will never happen. Find a new goal in life." Then I strutted away. I think I taught that guy a lesson.

Okay, okay, so I have a vivid imagination. That is not what really happened, but let's just say that was what I wanted to do. I didn't hurt his "package," but everything else happened just like I described. I never did find out what happened with the bet. Who got the money? Did someone bet that I would not have sex? If so, maybe I should thank him.

Although this wasn't the first time a boy had tried to get me to compromise my morals, this was the first time one had been so overt about his dirty little scheme. The teasing and bets quickly escalated. Daily I was singled out and ridiculed by guys who thought my standards were stupid. Sometimes I cried in the bathroom at school when no one was near and I often went home sad. I prayed fervently for the day to come when I wouldn't be made fun of for my standards. Little did they know that their constant teasing and the nights I spent crying over the continuous badgering made me more confident in my decision and secure in my stance.

High School Boys

Like every girl in junior high, I went through a shy stage. Mine just happened to last through high school. In high school, I was convinced that guys were only joking when they asked me out. Poor guys, I must have hurt their feelings. I said "No, thank you," when they asked me on a date, the whole time thinking that they were just asking me out to get a good laugh. Even after guys wrote in my yearbook, "I really like you and I think we should go out sometime," I still wasn't convinced that they were serious.

In high school I went on a couple of dates and to school dances. I wanted a boyfriend, I just didn't think I had time for one. I had dreams of playing college golf and becoming a professional athlete and I didn't want any distractions. My high school was only a few blocks away from the University of Colorado and I quickly fell in love with the gorgeous campus, awesome football team, and fun environment—I couldn't wait to become a Buffalo. I had scholarship offers at other universities, but I turned them down. I worked my butt off for the opportunity to play golf at the University of Colorado, a Division I NCAA college, and it finally happened.

College Guys

I started college a few years after the University of Colorado's football team won the national championship. So my freshman year, the football team was still coming off the high of winning the title, and preseason polls ranked the University of Colorado fourth in the nation. This was a huge deal. The entire state shut down on game day, tuned to ESPN, hung their football flags, watched both pre- and postgame shows, and hung on every word uttered by both the coach and quarterback.

I remember my first introduction to college life . . . ahh, being single never felt so good. It was as if my mom had visited the frat houses and the sports teams a week before school started and paid guys to ask me out. I never felt more desirable. The first week of school, the athletic department hosted a mandatory barbecue for the athletes as a way for us to get to know each other. I thought the athletic director deserved a raise for that idea. By the looks of the men walking into the party, I must have been blushing before I even got out of the car. Being a little awestruck, I did the first thing I always do at a party—smile, nod hello to a few people, and head straight for the food. I was so nervous. It was a little hard to breathe too. There were so many good-looking men at this event! (Praise God for barbeque and handsome men!) My high school had a handful of guys that I thought were attractive. This was a completely different scene.

At the party, athletic, good-looking men invaded the place like ants on picnic leftovers; they were everywhere. That's when I first noticed the quarterback, Jeremy. Jeremy was a six foot two, 210-pound cowboy from Texas with a muscular build and tight jeans. He rocked those jeans, if you know what I mean. At the time I didn't know who he was, I just thought he was cute. I looked down to pick out my second piece of chocolate cake, and when I looked back up, he was staring in my direction. Like any normal girl who had a hand-some jock looking at her, I turned around to see who he was looking at. Don't get me wrong, I thought I was cute, but not *that* cute, so why was he staring at me? My past experiences with guys definitely didn't prepare me for this, so I assumed that he must be looking at one of the volleyball players standing behind me. Later I found out that he just thought *I* was cute.

The athletic department mandated a ten-hour minimum of study hall each week for freshmen athletes. So, when I wasn't on the golf course, working out, in class, or sleeping, my free time was spent in study hall. Luckily, study hall was located in the same build-ing as the football offices. Life was rough . . . I *had* to study every night with gorgeous men all around me. One night while studying, Jeremy walked into study hall looking for a friend, but once he saw me he headed my way. (I knew all of my studying would pay off one day!) As soon as he started talking to me I forgot 99 percent of the material I spent the last hour memorizing. Ideally, I was supposed to clock in two more hours of studying for that night, but I had to eat sometime, right? How many times in a girl's life does she get asked out by the college quarterback? For now, homework could wait—I was asked out for sushi.

Shortly after that night, Jeremy and I went on several dates. If in high school you would have told me that my freshman year in college I would be dating the college quarterback, I would have laughed at you. You don't go from being a little, pony-tailed girl who plays golf and spends all her free time studying to dating the quarterback at a nationally ranked university. This wasn't a small community college—this was the big leagues. It was as if I were a modern-day Cinderella and Jeremy my handsome prince. He had a nationally recognized name, he was on major television networks during football season, he had his choice of more than fourteen thousand women on campus, and he was interested in *me*.

I always introduce my guy friends and potential boyfriends to my family, so, one night Jeremy came to my parents' house for dinner. Even after going on several fun dates with him, Jeremy still made me nervous. I wanted to impress him with my cooking skills, so I prepared shish kabobs, rice, salad, and a dessert. Normally, this meal is easy to cook, but that night, I burned the first batch of rice and the second batch was mushy. By then everyone was so hungry they wouldn't let me try a third time. Jeremy tried encouraging me by saying, "It's not that bad," but just as the soggy rice filled his mouth like a bag of warm marshmallows, he muffled, "Mmm, I lub mushy lice." My family lost it and we all started laughing. So much for trying to win his heart with my culinary skills.

Later that night Jeremy and I went to see *The Horse Whisperer*. At one point during the movie, as the camera zoomed in on the Montana landscape of horses, fields, and ranches, Jeremy leaned over and whispered, "Do you think you could ever settle down in a place like that?" *Settle down? Is he thinking about us being together in the future, about us getting married? Shoot, I might live anywhere with you, cowboy.* I tried to respond in a way that hid my excitement and nervousness and said,

"Only if there is a golf course nearby." He smiled and we continued watching the movie. Throughout the movie he made similar comments, and near the end I was more convinced than ever that Jeremy was a charmer. You know the kind, the more they talk the more you want to cuddle up with them. I wanted to reach over and plant one on him. That night I noticed Jeremy making conscious efforts to open up and let me get to know him better. It was wonderful and sweet.

Although Jeremy and I had talked about God before, on the ride home I felt God prompting me to talk more with Jeremy about what it really means to put your faith in God. I tried negotiating with God, because though I was normally bold about sharing my faith, this time I had a weird feeling that if I shared my faith with this cowboy quarterback, he would never call me again. It was as if God was asking me to trust Him with my dating life, to trust Him to provide for my romantic needs even if Jeremy wasn't the one for me. So I mustered my courage, shared my faith, and spoke the truth about God.

As I began speaking, I knew I was saying goodbye to my fantasies about my future with Jeremy. They were good fantasies too! Like the *SportsCenter* highlight clips of Jeremy blowing me kisses from the field just before a major third-down conversion, or Jeremy proposing to me on the scoreboard during halftime. It sounds crazy, but I know I am not the only girl with Cinderella dreams. After I shared my heart with Jeremy, we never went out again. We didn't really talk much either. I was sad, but I was content because I was obedient to God and I knew God was protecting me.

Still, there was just something about him. *Why do I think about this guy so much? I want to date a man who is passionate about living for and loving God, and Jeremy is not it.* Jeremy, like most cowboys, drove a diesel truck. I thought about him so much that every time I heard a diesel truck, I turned to see if it was him. I prayed day and night that God would take this quarterback, my temptation, far away from me. Less than one week later, a front-page story informed everyone that our NCAA quarterback suddenly transferred to Texas A&M. I know the Bible says that God answers prayers, but dang, I didn't imagine that he would move Jeremy to another state! Well, like any football team minus a quarterback, our team played terribly that year. We were 4–4 in our conference. All my friends on the golf team blamed me for the horrible football season.

The Good Single Life

After my freshman year in college, I went from dating three guys a week to dating one guy every five years. Despite my constant self-affirmations that I am "living the good single life," my sensitivity and arousal to sex (and all the pleasures that accompany it) has radically increased. Because I have been single for so long, I try convincing myself that with my continued abstinence I will eventually grow calloused to my sexual desires (until I am married, of course). It only makes sense that God would take away my sexual desires until I am able to act on them in a way that pleases the Lord, in marriage. But so far, I haven't felt any callousness. Nope. None here. If anything, the more time that passes, the more intense my cravings for sex become.

With the increasing sensual surges of heat and pleasure that shoot through my body, daily I am reminded that I was created by God to engage in sexual acts. Immediately after that thought, I remember that I am still single. Here's the thing: I am a single virgin and the only thing I can do to change this fact, according to Scripture, is to have sex with my husband. I am not overly anxious to rush into marriage with just anyone, so I continue to wait.

I have tried focusing on living the "good single life" like all the popular books encouraged. I even "said goodbye to dating" for a while. Depending on the book, I followed the six or ten steps to finding a godly Christian man or being single and satisfied. You name it, I tried it, but with only temporary success. Just when I would think I could coast through my singleness, I would find myself alone, wanting companionship, and really, really wanting sex. I know I don't just want *sex*; I want a lifetime commitment of marriage with a man who I admire, love, cherish, and satisfy. I want to know what sex feels like. I want to have sex in places that take imagination. I want to become one with my man as God commands a husband and wife to unite in shameless oneness. Meanwhile, I wait and I pray and I try very hard to focus my thoughts on things that will glorify God. It just so happens that picturing a man naked isn't one of those things, at least not at this stage in my life. So what happened to me? Growing up I thought that sex was gross. I didn't want to talk about it, I didn't want to hear about it, and I definitely didn't want to see pictures of genitalia. Now? Now I find it hard to sleep at night without waking up halfway through another enticing and imaginative sexual dream. Argh! Why is this happening to me? Sweet church girls aren't supposed to think about sex, are they?

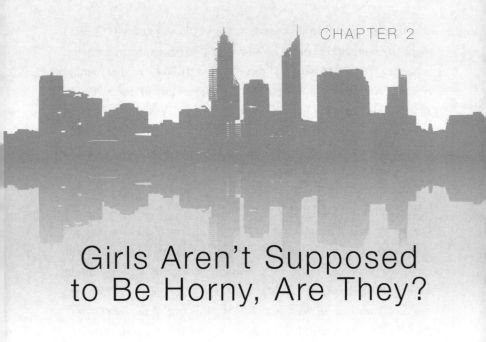

CHAPTER 2

Girls Aren't Supposed to Be Horny, Are They?

I HAVE REALIZED THAT I'VE BEEN CHEATED and I am pretty ticked off about it. I think I deserve a rewind. I should get to go back to, say, the eighth grade and have someone, *anyone*, tell me that I would grow up to be an extremely horny virgin. This isn't asking too much, is it? Everyone knows that *guys* are sexual minded, but no one ever told me that *I* would feel this way too.

Maybe my frustration comes from the fact that I am a planner. I don't need to control what's going to happen; I just want to know the plan. If we are going to hang out, play Yahtzee, watch a movie—cool, I'm good with that. If we are going on vacation a year from now—great, I'll enter it into my iPhone. In sixth grade my P.E. teacher told me that for the next three or four years, guys would grow older and taller and would act like idiots, so just ignore them. My mom's friends said that guys would think about sex a lot; it was normal. Great, I made my notes and planned on it so that I was not surprised when it happened. But hello! No one, I mean NO ONE, told me that I would be out of control horny like those teenage boys. I guess I never thought about it either. At the time, I thought an unequal sex drive in men and women was God's way of keeping the population low or something. Now that I am fully aware that girls lust too, what am I supposed to do? I wasn't prepared for this.

I Wasn't Prepared for This

Due to my lack of preparation for this stage in my life, I have resigned to running out of buildings and even Bible studies when I can't handle my sexual cravings. I can't keep doing this. Seriously, people might start to think that I am a little strange. Do you remember Potiphar's wife and the incident with Joseph? Joseph is one of my heroes from the Old Testament and I think we have a lot in common. Although I have never had someone's spouse grab me by my shirt and say "Lie with me!" I have had several guys offer sex and everything else.

In the book of Genesis we read that Joseph's brothers sold him into slavery, and eventually he was purchased by Potiphar. Potiphar was an extremely wealthy officer in Pharaoh's service. After seeing how God blessed Joseph, Potiphar put him in charge of everything he owned (including his servants). The only thing that Potiphar withheld from Joseph was his wife. Makes sense. The Bible usually emphasizes inner beauty, but in Joseph's case, it mentioned that he had both integrity and good looks. Day and night Potiphar's wife tried to seduce Joseph into sex by saying, "Lie with me." One day Potiphar's wife grabbed Joseph by the shirt and said, "Lie with me," and he ran out of that house so fast that he left his shirt behind.

It wasn't until my senior year in college that I realized my desire for sex was off the charts. One minute I was singing along at a Christian concert, the next minute I was imagining doing sexual things with the guitar player. I didn't know what to do. I couldn't make it stop, so I picked up my purse, waved goodbye to my friends, and ran out of the building. The same thing still happens at Bible studies, barbeques, and date nights. What would have happened if I didn't leave immediately? I don't even want to think about that. Perhaps if I had been better informed, then I could have come up with a better plan. Maybe by following in Joseph's footsteps, I am taking Paul a little too seriously when he says, "Flee youthful lusts."[1] But what else am I supposed to do? So far, running away works for me.

Although I am not exactly sure how I would have planned on being a crazed, lustful, virgin, I would have done *something*. I could have researched how to avoid being sexually tempted or asked my married friends how they controlled their lust prior to marriage. I could have made lists of activities to subdue my sensual thoughts and feelings (at least until I am married). *Is that even possible?* Maybe it's not too late to start. Instead of taking an hour lunch break, I could break up my time and schedule four fifteen-minute ice-cold showers throughout the day. I know! I can go for long walks during lunch. Yes, walking will give me a way to release some of my built up sexual tension! *But wait; doesn't exercising produce more endorphins that will increase my sex drive?* If only I had advanced notice about this phase in my life . . . I would have found a way to marry before I turned eighteen. Gosh, being a virgin with an overactive sex drive is really frustrating.

Virginal Thoughts

Ever since I can remember I have tried to protect my mind and body from sexual images, messages, and experiences. I switched to country music at age thirteen when songs like "Let's Talk About Sex" started playing on the hip-hop stations. I rarely watch movies that have a rating higher than PG-13 because I can't handle those images rolling around in my head. I read my Bible almost daily and I really try to absorb the words. I listen to Christian music 24/7, but I still wake up in the middle of the night hot, sweaty, and ready for sex as Marvin Gaye's lyrics to "Let's Get It On" play nonstop in my head.

My first introduction to the opposite sex was in kindergarten when a boy in my class told me he wanted to kiss me during recess. *Gross, cooties.* Ever since then, I was convinced that boys were very odd. I wish I knew what flipped in my head. One minute I thought guys were disgusting, the next minute I was picturing having sex with one of them in my dorm room bunk bed.

I couldn't escape this sensual movie clip as it kept replaying in my head. One second I was studying for a test in my room—nothing out of the ordinary about that—and the next second I pictured myself having sex with one of the guys from my history class. Immediately I stopped my thoughts, opened my eyes, and stared at something, *anything*, to take my mind off the movie my imagination created. I asked God for forgiveness (for lusting and for enjoying my lustful thoughts) and tried to calm myself down. This thought lasted for less than three seconds, and yet I felt it through my entire body.

The next day in history class I couldn't even look at the guy. He was a tall, handsome basketball player who always had girls throwing themselves at him. In my efforts to keep my lustful fantasy to myself, I went out of my way to ignore him, just in case he tried to play those Jedi mind games on me. A couple weeks later he asked me out and I quickly declined his offer, thanked him, and headed for the library. I was confident that the library would be a better place for me to study—after all, who has sexual thoughts in a boring, stuffy, dingy library? After spending countless hours in our school library, I read that it was rated one of the best places in the state to meet your future spouse. Since I didn't want a replay of the bunk bed mind scene, I resumed studying alone in my bedroom, this time, minus the bunk beds.

Lucky for me, these are just my thoughts. No one can tell what I am thinking just by looking at me, right? Or can they? Like the time I was sitting on an airplane waiting for the flight attendants to open the cabin doors so we could exit. It was kind of fun to watch the airline personnel outside preparing the plane for the next flight. Everything was fine until the baggage handlers started unloading the luggage from below the aircraft. The noise it made was rhythmic and sounded like people having sex on a squeaky bed. The sound instantly reminded me of one of my former next-door neighbors. My roommate and I were talking in our room one night when suddenly we heard someone knocking on our wall. We were both curious, so my roommate, with a glass to her ear, quietly leaned against the wall to figure out who was knocking. We didn't need the glass for very long because the steady squeaking and thumping of the neighbor's bed against our wall let us know exactly what was happening.

I stood in the plane's aisle just as the squeaking began to crescendo. I swear I felt the plane slightly rocking. I wanted to shout, "Stop with the noises already!" *Seriously, I don't know how much more of this I can handle.* Instead I used my remaining energy to focus on something other than the noise. As I looked around at the people waiting to exit the plane, I wondered if they were thinking the same thing I was. It was apparent by their calm, bored faces that I was alone in my thoughts.

Maybe this is just a phase I am going through. I am usually good at controlling my thoughts. But lately, it seems that I can't go anywhere without thinking about getting naked and having sex. I was at Chipotle and I wanted a burrito without a tortilla. As it turns out, this menu item is called a "Naked Burrito." Great! *Thanks Chipotle.* I was in the grocery store buying vegetables, and as I turned the corner I saw a bottle of "Naked Juice" for sale right next to the sliced pineapple. As I was on the elliptical machine at the gym, I flipped through the TV channels and I heard a talk show host say something about "the naked truth." What is it with being naked? I am not safe anywhere—not even in the grocery store! I don't get it. Can't the truth just be the truth? Is truth more validated when it is naked? Call me old-fashioned, but why do burritos and juice need to be naked? Please, for the love of singles everywhere, call them anything but "naked." Is every unmarried female like me? Am I normal?

What's a Girl to Do?

Growing up I was taught the dos and don'ts of sex. Don't lust. Don't have sex. Don't go out with anyone your parents don't like. Do use the Bible for guidance and instruction. Do listen to your parents. Do wait until marriage to have sex. These rules were great for me, and they still are, but every year I realize that I need to be more specific about a few things. Instead of my parents adding rules to this list as I grew up, I did. Since then I have become more aware of my sensual and sexual limitations, and I am not afraid to put myself in "time-out," or whatever else I need to do to help me live a pure lifestyle.

Recently my list of dos and don'ts became more complicated than before. Don't kiss my boyfriend for more than thirty seconds continually. Don't lie next to him when we kiss. Don't kiss his ear; it makes me think about giving in to my indulgences. Don't listen to certain songs; they get me turned on very, very quickly. When the baggage people are unloading the luggage after a flight, don't think about having sex. And don't seduce people in my dreams.

Even with the list, being sexually pure is really, really difficult sometimes. After all, the Bible says, "There is none righteous, not even one," "The spirit is willing, but the flesh is weak," and "The heart is more deceitful than all else."[2] *God, how am I supposed to live a holy and pure life in a culture that makes fun of virgins and makes it hard to be one? Please, help me, God. I can't do this on my own.* Looking back, I wish my prayer was more specific than simply, "God, please help me." Sometimes, well, most times, I don't understand what God is up to and I don't always like the way God "helps" me in my time of need. What I had in mind when I prayed this was one of two things: God would just make me stronger, or He would delay my desires until the day I say, "I do." But that is not how it happened.

I Can't Get No . . . Satisfaction

The Bible says that it is better to marry than to burn with lust.[3] I am all for that, but what is a girl to do? Paul was likely writing to men who could choose to take a wife at a time when it was unheard of for a woman to choose a husband. Marital circumstances haven't changed much, unless you are J-Lo or Demi Moore.

Just like all of my single girlfriends, I have a lot to offer a guy in a romantic relationship. So why are we still single? Based on my interactions with guys, I have concluded that either they have issues, or they are shy. Over the past few years I have been interested in a few guys, but for some reason they barely said hello to me, let alone asked me out. For the past four years, my mom (who is also my best friend) and I have taken mental notes of how guys respond to me. After living in Colorado and attending the same church for more than a year, it was like pulling teeth to get guys to say hi to me during the "meet and greet" portion of the service. Seriously, am I asking too much by expecting guys to say hi to me after I greet them with a hello? One day as the worship band finished, the pastor took center stage and told us to introduce ourselves to those sitting around us. So, being the good, church-attending Christian that I am, I turned around and introduced myself to people. On this particular Sunday I turned around and there was a guy—around my age—standing in the row behind me. I extended my hand and said, "Hi, nice to meet you. My name is Lindsey." I thought I was friendly and sincere. I bathed that day, my fingernails were slightly polished, I was wearing a cute outfit, and I had even sprayed a touch of perfume. So, you can believe my astonishment when he looked me in the eyes, muffled a "hlo," turned around without shaking my hand, and proceeded to talk to his friends sitting behind him. *Are you serious?*

I ran into this guy at another church event and our second interaction was similar to the first.

Another time the church put together a Coffee House night as an opportunity for new people to mingle with others from the church who were in Bible studies. It was a perfect way for someone like me (who didn't really know anyone in the church) to get connected and make new friends. I was standing next to the dessert table, talking with my buddy, Pastor Gene, when I noticed this guy walking back and forth at the dessert table. I love to people watch, so this guy's peculiar behavior promised to be entertaining. On the table sat ten different cheesecakes, individually boxed. He moved from the left side of the table to the right side, opening and closing each box as he passed. Open, close, open, close, open, close. He was probably looking for a particular dessert. But when he reached the end of the table and started moving from the right to left, repeating the same motions of opening and closing each box, I realized that maybe he was trying to figure out the flavors of each cheesecake. As he moved down the row of boxes, I noticed that the name of the cheesecake was written on the inside lid of each box. I thought it would be funny to act as if he didn't know what type of dessert he was looking at. So, I leaned forward and said to him, "It's cheesecake." He turned around and said, "No, I, uh . . . I know . . . ," then he walked away without completing his sentence. *Who does that? At least say something witty in response.*

Maybe shy or weird guys are God's way of protecting me from temptation. After all, it is extremely difficult to be tempted to have sex when you can't even get the guy in the row behind you to reciprocate a cordial "hello." Although this wasn't how I envisioned my "help," I still praise God for keeping me pure.

It's Not About Me

As I mentioned earlier, Joseph is a hero of mine. Looking at the whole of his life, he must have had more than a few years when he thought God's "help" wasn't all that helpful. Like the time when Joseph's brothers were planning to kill him, but instead sold him as a slave. "God's ways are not our ways" is a common saying, and it is so true.[4] The way God does things is usually not the way I would do things. Probably the best way to keep me and others pure was to keep all the men far, far away from me. Possibly the best way to save an entire population from starvation was to allow Joseph's brothers to sell him into slavery.

Remember the story of Joseph's refusal to sleep with his boss's wife? One day after refusing her advances once again, she accused him of attempted rape, and Joseph was thrown into prison. Let's just say that his prison experience was nothing like that of Martha Stewart or Paris Hilton. His prison term had no limits, no guarantees, no toilets, and no wi-fi. I am talking about the type of prison where prisoners were either chained to a guard, a wall, or both. This was the kind of place where prisoners ate out of the cup they peed in, and excreted in the corner they slept in. I'm not sure that Joseph was really "thanking God" for His "help" at that point. Talk about a difficult situation. It doesn't seem fair. As far as the Bible tells us, Joseph's life pleased the Lord. So why was Joseph being punished for doing what was right? Why does it sometimes feel like I am being punished when I too have tried to do what's right by living a sexually pure lifestyle?

Joseph wasn't perfect, but his perspective was: love and obey God, every day in every situation. Instead of getting wrapped up in the heat of the moment when he had a woman begging him for sex, Joseph chose to do what was right. What he said to Potiphar's wife was so profound that his words often echo in my head: "How then could I do this great evil and sin against God?"[5] *I love that!* I could come up with a list of things that I would say or have said to someone wanting sex from me. But all my reactions aside, the real reason why I wouldn't indulge in my sexual desires can be summed up in

Joseph's simple, sagacious statement. Joseph didn't want to harm his relationship with God.

We read that even when Joseph was sold by his family, became a slave, and was wrongly accused and imprisoned, God was with Joseph.[6] Through those hard years, God blessed Joseph and gave him favor with his leaders. Joseph was created by God, and although it didn't look like it while he was a slave or in prison, God had a special plan for Joseph's life. By looking at Joseph's actions, we can infer that he was able to see past his situation and realize that his life was not about him. This concept is one of the easiest to forget and the most difficult to execute. *It's not about me. My life is not about me.*

Throughout my life I have been asked repeatedly, "Why are you still a virgin?" My answer has always resembled Joseph's: "I don't want to sin against God." I want to be clear that virgins are not perfect! I most definitely am not perfect. Daily I am reminded that I have a long way to go, but just as Joseph was blessed for his obedience, I have experienced many blessings from living a sexually pure lifestyle. I can honestly say that I would forgo any sexual experience for the opportunity to become closer to God. *It's not about me.*

Since the "sex talk" my sophomore year in college, I have eagerly sought biblical answers to my sex questions. I couldn't rest until I knew if God was for or against dating, foreplay, flirting, living with my boyfriend, sex, and a host of other issues. What if I don't like sex with my husband? What if what everyone else says is true; what if I am missing out by waiting? But what if I am making the right decisions, the best decisions? What if my decisions are pleasing to God? Even though virgins are few and far between, maybe I still can make a difference. Maybe I can remind others of God's promises for those who save sex for marriage. I entreat you to join me as I wrestle with these topics and try to live a life that pleases God.

CHAPTER 3

You're Missing Out!

AFTER GRADUATING FROM COLLEGE, my roommate Annadee and I moved to San Diego and began adjusting to the new city and city life. We quickly discovered that our quaint apartment in a nice neighborhood wasn't as charming as we had hoped. One night while sleeping, our R.E.M. cycles were drastically interrupted by curious sounds coming from our next-door neighbor's apartment. It wasn't long before Annadee and I realized that our neighbors were having sex. We were shocked, nervous, and giddy all at the same time, so we did the only natural thing that women in their early twenties do . . . we started laughing. We were laughing so hard, we covered our faces with pillows. Since we could hear them, they could probably hear us. I kept the pillow over my head and prayed that I would quickly fall asleep, because by the sounds of it, sex seemed pretty exciting.

Every day millions and millions of singles are having sex. When people ask me why I haven't had sex yet, it's easy to wonder, *why am*

I still waiting for sex when I could have sex right now? My entire life people have tried to convince me that I am "missing out" because I haven't had sex yet. It has taken me a while to see their point of view, but I am finally ready to admit that they are right: *I am missing out!*

I Am Missing Out on Seven-Minute "Love"

Throughout high school and college, my friends had sex with their boyfriends because they thought they were in love. As I observed my friends' relationships, I noticed that for a while, each boyfriend seemed like the perfect guy. He called her when he missed her, wrote her love notes and gave them to her as they passed in the hall, brought her flowers, stayed late after football games just to talk to her . . . it seemed like he was perfect. I admit I was kind of jealous of some of those girls. I wanted a guy to blow me kisses from across the lunchroom, put my picture in his locker, and walk down the hall with his arm around me. Who wouldn't want that kind of attention from a guy?

I never knew all the details, but it was usually a couple of months after she had sex with him that the relationship started to change. He smiled as she walked by instead of walking with her, flirted with other girls to make her jealous, and invited other girls to dances. Now my friends' exes have been reduced to a list of guys' names they slept with. Many of these girls thought they were in love, so what went wrong? Sex *can* be a way to show someone you love them, but only when that sex occurs inside a marriage between a husband and wife. Outside of a marriage relationship, sex is selfish and the wrong way to show someone you care for them. Some researchers say that as little as seven minutes after having sexual relations with a girl, the guy is looking for something else, or someone else to "do."[1] Seven minutes! I can't even fix my hair in seven minutes. *Seven minutes,* you've got to be joking. Most girls after having sex probably spend the first thirty minutes just wondering if he thought she was fat, or if she was "good," and hoping that he loved her more because she had sex with him. But after having sex, he is most likely thinking about something completely opposite of that. He is probably not thinking about you at all.

I saw something like this happen at a fraternity party I attended in college. I walked into a room that was dimly lit. A few guys offered me something to drink, and as I said "No, thanks" I saw a guy stand up from behind the couch at the end of the room, adjust his clothes, and walk past me with a bottle of something in his hand. *That was strange*, I thought. *I didn't know anyone was over there.* About five minutes after he left the room, I saw a college girl stand up from behind that same couch, adjust her clothes, and exit the room. Obviously I wanted to leave this place, but I was with people who weren't done partying yet. Yeah, some party. I never saw those two together the rest of the night.

I don't know about you, but I am not looking for the kind of "love" that lasts seven minutes, a week, a month, or a year. I want the kind of love from a man that makes him want to be committed to me for life. I deserve a man who will show me he loves me, not someone who simply talks about loving me. Real love can be seen in the man who sacrifices his needs and desires to bless and serve you, in hopes of helping you in your relationship with Jesus.[2] Real love can be seen in the guy who lets you eat the rest of his sandwich even when he is still hungry, and thinks you're beautiful even when your hair is messy and all your makeup is wiped off. Real love is found in a man who values your opinions and takes the time to understand who you are and what you think. Real love is the kind that defends you when others say hurtful things. It's in a man who offers you his shirt because he thinks it will help keep you warm. He is someone who pledges his whole life to loving and serving you, and he's faithful and keeps his promises. When a man loves you for who you are, he doesn't try to change you, and his motives for being nice to you are pure.

A loving man listens to you, encourages you, and searches for new ways to show you he cares. Real love is in a man who doesn't want to live one more day without everyone in the world knowing that you are his wife. He doesn't abandon you because of an argument or focus only on the difficulties of the relationship, but desires to provide a committed marriage environment that is safe and trustworthy for you and your future kids. Real love is simply that: real. It's not some Hollywood fantasy relationship where people don't talk about real issues, real pain, or real feelings because when the love is real, so are the benefits and consequences.

The Hollywood culture promotes the mentality that "If you really love a person, then you should have sex with that person." In our relativistic, "If it feels good, do it," and "What happens in Vegas, stays in Vegas" society that refuses any absolutes (especially those that speak against promiscuous relationships), where should we draw the line? The line that I am talking about is this: God mandates absolute rights and wrongs about who, what, when, where, and why to have sex. Each romantic relationship has a time and place for sex to occur; that time and place is between a husband and his wife. Acting in ways that satisfy our sexual desires outside of this type of marriage relationship, especially at the expense of others, is not love, but lust.

If you are defining sex outside of marriage as love, then you're right, I am "missing out." Not only am I missing out on that kind of "love," I'm missing out on wondering if the guy I'm dating really likes me, or if he's just dating me for sex. I am missing out on being heartbroken because I was sexually close with someone, hoping it would bring us emotionally closer, only to have it tear us apart. I am missing out on the hurt and regret that comes once you realize what you gave away. I am missing out on having the reputation of being a slut, makeout partner, hook-up buddy, or someone who will have sex after a cheap dinner date. I'm missing out on waking up in a fraternity house the morning after a party, wondering where I am and who the man is lying next to me. Did we have sex? If so, did I have sex with more than one person? Did I enjoy *any* of it?

Contrary to popular opinion, sex does *not* equal love, and love does *not* equal sex. If sex equaled love and love equaled sex, then prostitutes would be the happiest and most "loved" people on the planet. After all, they have more sex than anyone else. Yet you don't have to live too long to know that you won't find a picture of a prostitute in the dictionary when you look up the words *love* or *happy*. The Bible mentions the word *sex* (or its equivalent) almost 80 times and the word *love* almost 700 times. If God thought that we were supposed to show guys (who we aren't married to) that we love them by having sex with them, don't you think He would have mentioned this in at least *one* of the 780 verses that include the words *sex* or *love*? In fact, it's just the opposite. God commands singles to abstain from sexual thoughts and actions, and yet He commands husbands and wives to enjoy the pleasures and benefits of sex within their marriage relationship.

People tell me I am missing out on love, happiness, and the pure enjoyment that comes from having sex outside of marriage. But I'm not interested in fulfilling a guy's sexual desire only to be left with a broken heart, a bad reputation, shattered dreams, mixed emotions, and confusion. I don't ever want a guy to show me that he "loves" me like that. That's not what I am looking for.

I Am Missing Out on Mediocre Sex

Can I be Captain Obvious for a second? Okay, because I am remaining a virgin until I get married, this means I have not and will not have sex until marriage. By not having sex until I am married, I will have potentially missed out on a lot of sex. But at least I know that I'll have good sex when I am married. Think about it: For thousands of years people have saved sex for marriage. Why would anyone wait so long for sex if the sex with their spouse ended up being bad? If every person who married as a virgin thought sex was bad, it would take about, oh, I don't know, *two seconds* for everyone to find out about it. Right? I know a lot of men and women who were virgins when they were married and no one, and I mean no one, has said the sex was bad. Not one of them regretted waiting.

Now let me address a not-so-obvious topic. The majority of sexually active singles aren't having amazing sex. They aren't even having *good* sex. In multiple surveys, singles rated their sexual experiences as *mediocre*. Contrary to popular belief, the best sex is experienced by married couples, not singles.[3] Married couples rated their sex lives as "very exciting" compared to singles who said their sex was more like "business as usual." Forty-eight percent of single women polled admitted to faking an orgasm.[4] Forty-eight percent! That's a whole lot of pretending. David Gudgel writes,

> Contrary to popular belief, the best sex is not experienced by unmarried people. The National Sex Survey of 3,500 people and another survey of 1,000 people concluded that married people have more sex and better sex than singles do. A husband and wife have sex more often and enjoy it more than those who are unmarried. A long-term marital commitment deepens emotional and physical satisfaction, even over decades of marriage. Studies by Dr. Evelyn Duvall and Dr. Judson Landis resulted in the same conclusion: Premarital sex is not as satisfying as marital sex. Sexual happiness is also connected to whether or not a couple saves sex for marriage. Those who do wait are 29 to 47 percent more likely to enjoy it within marriage. The Family Research Council found that 72 percent of these couples report higher sexual satisfaction.[5]

Does it surprise you that married couples have better sex than singles? Sex sounds exciting and rewarding in a marriage relationship, and if you ask me, it makes perfect sense. Sure it sounds adventurous to have sex with someone on the first date, someone you just met in a bar, or a hot guy from one of your classes—for a second that sounds fun. But as often as people "hook up" and try to subdue their feelings of wanting a commitment from their sexual partners, I can only conclude that they maintain and increase their sexual activity in search of the connection, security, and happiness that married couples have. They take and give sex searching for "great sex" and many times, love. They settle for mediocre sex when they could actually be holding out for great sex. It is no surprise to me that the way God says to "do it" (pun intended), is constantly supported by research as being the best way.

I am missing out on a lot by not having sex until I'm married, and I thank God that I am missing out! After waiting thirty years to have sex, I want to be sure that I'll have *fun, exciting,* and *exhilarating* sex when I'm married! Despite what people may think I am missing out on, I will continue to hold fast to my convictions, all the while praying for my husband to come along. Really, I just need one guy. One godly, funny, *fine* guy!

I Am Missing Out on Clinic Exams

I used to volunteer at a pregnancy center. One day around noon, instead of eating lunch, I sat in the lobby and waited for my boss. As I looked around the room I saw brochures that explained what to do if you have an STI[6] and positive options to explore if you find out you are pregnant (i.e., support groups, financial resources, and adoption). As I sat there, I thanked God that I never had to come to this room because of my sexual choices. I wondered what it must be like to come here.

Women come to this waiting room to find answers. They come

to find out if they are pregnant or have an STI. The girls are afraid to tell anyone about their concerns. They don't want to ask their moms to buy them a pregnancy test, or they don't trust themselves to get an accurate reading from a pregnancy test. As I sat in the waiting room, I pictured young, single girls hearing the words, "You're pregnant," and seeing their tears as they tried to cope with their new reality. Then I remembered praying for five years for my friend and her husband to be blessed enough to hear those same words from her doctor.

My thoughts were interrupted by a teenage girl who walked into the clinic waiting room. She was probably no older than fourteen. She sat there anxiously. I smiled at her in hopes of offering some sort of comfort. She smiled back and looked to the ground. I tried to think of something to say to her, but what do you say to a girl in *this* waiting room? My mind raced with questions as I too looked at the floor. When I saw the anxiety in her facial expressions, I became nosey and wanted to know if she was sleeping with her boyfriend or if her visit here was the result of a one-night stand. How old was she? Did her parents know that she was sexually active? Were they even aware that she was interested in boys? It wasn't any of my business, and I didn't want to make her uncomfortable by asking questions, so I was glad when her counselor called her back. That day in the waiting room broke my heart, but what kills me is knowing that this scene is replayed by millions of girls every year. Then a thought occurred to me: *No one should have to spend their lunch break here.*

SEXUALLY TRANSMITTED INFECTIONS

Despite the condom, contraceptive, and "sex education" push over the past decade, more than 54,000 people each day (27,000 between the ages of 15 and 24) and around 20 million people each year are infected with a *new* STI.[7] Pharmaceutical companies have created pills, shots, and patches to prevent some of the major

STIs, but like condoms, none of these methods are able to provide complete protection. Three STIs—Human Papillomavirus (HPV), Trichomoniasis, and Chlamydia—accounted for 88 percent of all new cases of STIs among those ages fifteen to twenty-four. I don't know what is scarier, the large number of STIs per year, or the fact that most of those teens showed no sign of an infection.[8] Get this: almost every individual diagnosed with an STI did *not* get proper treatment during the early stages of acquiring the STI simply because they didn't know they had an infection. This scares me because many STIs have harmful long-term effects on a woman's body.

For many reasons, condom supporters and distributors fail to mention condoms' failure to provide 100 percent protection against certain STIs and pregnancy.[9] When tested in laboratory conditions by lab technicians in fully lit rooms, in the ideal temperatures for condom exposure, condoms have only a 70 percent success rate. As one condom supporter said, "Condoms are the best imperfect way we have."[10] But condom makers don't tell consumers about the imperfect success rate, nor do they openly state that a condom "may not" protect against STIs like HPV, which can be spread through skin-to-skin contact, or the HIV/AIDS virus.[11] If you want to gamble with getting herpes, HPV, Chlamydia, and over twenty-two other major STIs that can affect the genital and throat areas, then use "the best imperfect way" available. However, if your health is important to you, abstain from sex *and* sexual activity until marriage and remain faithful to your spouse. Otherwise you risk exposing yourself to infections.

PREGNANCY

STIs are scary, painful, and can leave a woman with a disease or condition for life, but that is not the only physical consequence that you can encounter while having sex outside of marriage. Each year in the United States, there are approximately 6 million pregnancies.

Out of those pregnancies, there are around 4 million live births and around 2 million pregnancy losses. Within the 2 million losses, around 600,000 women have a miscarriage and around 1,200,000 women choose termination.[12] Approximately 750,000 girls ages fifteen to nineteen become pregnant.[13] A 2002 report found that 29 percent of teenage girls who became pregnant chose to abort their baby.[14] I believe that there are a few main reasons why so many people condone abortions. Abortion appears to be a "quick fix" to a "messy" situation with little or no harm to anyone; the parents are afraid and don't think there is any other option; individuals don't believe that the fetus is actually a baby, a human being.

During my senior year in college, in order to complete my minor in Ethnic Studies, I took an African dance class. It was amazing! Learning a new culture through music and dance is fascinating. During the course of the semester I became good friends with a couple of girls in that class, one of whom I was paired with for the final dance project. My friend and I practiced all the time; we wanted our performance to be the best. One night while practicing she told me about a guy she had been dating for a while. I was caught off guard because she never even hinted that she was interested in anyone. The guy she was dating was from another country and . . . the rest of the conversation was like a bad dream. They had dated for a couple months, slept together, and now she was pregnant. He loved her and loved the fact that she was pregnant. He was excited about having a baby with her. She was only twenty-one and she was freaking out thinking about marrying an older man from another country . . . what would her parents say? Well, she thought they would kill her. She didn't know if she loved him, and she definitely wasn't sure that she wanted him around for the rest of her life. It appeared that having a romantic relationship with this man was sort of a "fun thing to do," but it became much more than that when she realized she was pregnant. That night I talked to her about her options and how abortion should not be one of them, but she didn't seem convinced. We danced some more. Before she left that night, I made her promise me that she wouldn't do anything without talking to me first. She promised, and I was relieved.

About a week or two went by and it seemed that she was back to her "normal" self, but then one Saturday I couldn't stop thinking about her. I don't remember what I was doing, but I felt like God was prompting me to pray for her . . . I felt like something bad was happening. I tried to call her, but I couldn't reach her. She had mentioned in our previous conversation that a friend of hers told her about a clinic in Denver, the kind that performed abortions, and I suddenly felt sick. *What am I supposed to do? I don't know where that clinic is. Am I supposed to drive around Denver hoping to find her?* I prayed and I prayed. I prayed for her and her baby. I didn't know exactly what I could do to help support her through her pregnancy, but I was sure I could find help. I never heard back from her, so I just kept calling until I finally reached her. I told her what happened to me on Saturday and asked her what she did that day. She was silent for a long time, then I heard muffled crying. Once she finally spoke, she kept repeating the same thing over and over: "Lindsey, why didn't you keep trying? I wish you would have gotten ahold of me . . ." By then I knew what had happened and I didn't know what to say, so I said nothing. She continued, "After it was over [she couldn't even say the word 'abortion'], they showed me my baby. Lindsey, it was my baby. It was the cutest thing ever; it had tiny arms and legs and it was so perfect . . . I wish you would have gotten ahold of me. I didn't believe that it was a baby, my baby."

This friend of mine, like many people, didn't believe (until it was too late) that a fetus is a human being.

Alternately, I have walked alongside women who have raised their babies without the father. It is possible to raise a child as a single mother, but it's not what God had in mind for the woman or the baby. I have cried many tears in agony when friends have called me telling me that they found out they have an STI. When we find out that we are not as invincible as we thought, when our consequences catch up with our poor sexual choices, it's painful.

In high school and college, I spent my lunch hour hanging out with friends, eating nachos, playing cards, and watching movies on Fridays in our cafeteria. I can think of *plenty* of other things I would rather be doing on my lunch break than sitting in a clinic waiting room . . . What do you spend your lunch breaks doing? What are you missing out on?

CHAPTER 4

Nude Beaches and My Curiosity

I WAS AN ART MAJOR for a couple of semesters in college. During my painting course, just before our final assignment, we were supposed to paint a person. This scared me, because I could paint bushes and Yoda, but people? I wasn't so sure. My professor said we would have a model join us for a few classes. Now I don't know what picture comes to your mind when you hear the word *model*, but if you are anything like me, you are picturing an Armani model with a five o'clock shadow. As you can imagine, after a week of anticipating our model, I was pretty excited when the day finally arrived. I even freshened up my makeup before class, just in case. I set up my easel and painting station like always, talked with my friends, and then noticed a new guy in class. *This must be our model,* I thought. He was thin with dark hair, pale skin color, and a little on the hairy side.

Nothing like what I pictured. Maybe it's for the best. I wasn't sure how I was expected to get any painting done if an Armani model actually showed up in our class.

My professor introduced the model to the class and explained that he would sit in the same position every day so we could paint an accurate portrait. *Funny outfit,* I thought as I noticed the model wearing a robe over his clothes. *Who wears a robe to school, especially when it's so nice outside? Whatever, it's Boulder. People dress kind of weird here . . . I wish I was an experienced painter. How am I going to paint a white robe and make it look interesting?* The model stood with his back toward me across the room. Then out of the corner of my eye, I saw him throw his robe to the ground and walk toward his chair . . . naked. The model was *naked!* My jaw dropped to the floor and I almost fell off my stool. *Whoa buddy, I did not sign up for this! I just want to learn how to paint. I don't need to see that stuff until I'm married! My professor could have warned me that our model would be a nude model.*

The blurred glimpse I got out of the corner of my eye was enough to make me feel like puking. To make matters worse, as horrifying as my glimpse was, I still thought about taking a second look. He sat down and sprawled himself across the sofa chair. His right leg dangled off of the armrest and his left leg rested comfortably on the chair. *Gosh this is awkward. Guys sit with their legs apart, I know, but dang, do your legs need to be that far apart?*

I quickly adjusted my easel to block my view of *all* of his genitalia. From my angle I could see the right side of the chair, his face, and his calf as it hung over the chair, which was perfect. *Whew, that was close! That was too close!* Although I was curious about what a man looks like naked, I didn't dare sneak any peeks. I was just relieved to find a viewing angle that didn't focus on his penis. *Hello, can you help a girl out? I gave myself a little pep talk: Lindsey, just breathe. Relax, it's just a guy and you are only painting his face, arm, and calf. Just pretend like he's wearing clothes and you'll be fine.*

My pep talk worked and I was able to regroup and focus on painting. But just as I applied the first colors to the canvas, my professor insisted that we all get up and walk in a circle around the room. "I want you all to make sure you have the best angle," he said. *Oh, thanks, how considerate of you.* Although I circled the room with the other students, I refused to look at the model. I didn't need to; I was perfectly content with painting the side of the chair. I had never seen a guy naked before and I was positive that I didn't want this guy to be my first. With all said and done, I made it through my painting class without seeing a naked guy, but this was a close call.

Just when I thought I had escaped a premature encounter with male nudity . . . the summer after my junior year in college, my family decided to vacation in Europe. Twenty family members, including my grandma, parents, sister, aunts, uncles, and cousins, went on a fourteen-day cruise through the Mediterranean. Our ports included France, Italy, Portugal, Gibraltar, and Morocco, to name a few. When I first heard about our trip, I had two major questions: Is the food on the ship really as good as people say it is, and does France really have nude beaches?

While sitting down to eat my rotisserie chicken at a French deli, I realized we had a full view of a nude beach. I am from Colorado, a place where it snows and is cold most of the year, so nude beaches were something new for me. Really, it sounds fun to go to a beach when you are picturing Matt Damon, Brad Pitt, or Shemar Moore walking around nude, but the French men I saw near the beaches looked nothing like those guys. It was when I saw two sixty-year-old, pale, white, chubby, hairy men walking to the beach, each with a towel around his waist, that I decided to skip the beach.

It wasn't until we left the French bistro that I realized my sex education was lacking. This got me thinking about what I knew about sex and where I learned it. With a little reflection, I realized that I never really learned about sex. From school I learned about female body parts and how women's bodies develop, at home I learned about abstinence, and in church I learned, well, nothing.

What We're Taught In School

My four-year-old nephew walked in on me as I was getting ready to get in the shower, and he said something appropriate for his age: "You don't have a penis. Only boys have a penis." Then he proceeded to say, "You have boobies, but my mom's boobies are bigger than yours." *Thanks, buddy. You could have skipped that last comment.* A few months later, my nephew started kindergarten, where he undoubtedly learned the differences between boys and girls.

In the fourth grade my classmates taught me about "going out" with boys, although you don't really go anywhere at all. I also learned that it's better to date someone who is around your height and weight, which was hard for me because I was taller than the boys my age. One day during recess my "boyfriend" asked me to sit on his lap. I looked at him like he was crazy and asked, "Are you sure?" He was shorter and smaller than me, but when he nodded, I sat on his lap and pretty much crushed him. After about a minute he asked me to sit next to him.

In eighth grade, when my teacher displayed pictures of a woman's body and a man's body and tried to explain words like *ovulation, clitoris, vagina, penis, semen, erection, acne,* and *puberty,* the co-ed class started giggling. I remember thinking, *Why didn't they split up the boys and girls for this lesson?* I didn't need to feel like all the guys in the room were staring at us girls as the teacher told them about our bodies. And I don't care how old you are, no one wants to hear their body parts described as "moist." That word should be banned from sex-ed curriculum.

In my tenth-grade health class I remember the teacher talking about STIs, mentioning names like *Chlamydia* (crabs), *Herpes* (the "gift" that keeps on giving), and other terms that most people couldn't pronounce. I remembered these words because my male classmates shared disgusting stories of their and others' sexual experiences, stories I wish I had never heard. The climax of the class was when our teacher grabbed a banana and proceeded to show us how to put a condom on it—pretending that it was a penis. *That is just plain weird.*

In college I was surprised to hear teachers openly share about their sexual experiences. One teacher told us that she had a neighbor complain to her boyfriend because she was too loud when they had sex. *TMI. Thanks for that bit of info that I did not want to hear.* Another teacher talked about how she hated Viagra and the service it offered men. That was when I raised my hand and told the class, "Look, I'm waiting to have sex until I am married. If my husband needs to use Viagra someday so we can continue to have fun and exciting sex no matter how old we get, then so be it." She quickly changed the subject.

This was the extent of my school education about sex. This sex education didn't provide what we ladies need to know about sex and sexual experiences. Sitting in a classroom listening to a teacher tell me about my sexual organs as she puts a condom on a banana is not exactly motivation to remain abstinent. Learning about the female anatomy is not sex education, and it definitely doesn't teach about the importance and value of sex and why we should wait until marriage. Furthermore, my sex-ed teachers were either single, divorced, or in second marriages. They were old, clueless about the teen scene, and needed to go on the show *What Not to Wear.* Through them and the media I learned what the world has to say about sex.

What We're Taught in the Media

In every imaginable form of communication, media encourages, entices, seduces, and allures people into having sex outside a marriage relationship. *Sex in the City, Lipstick Jungle, Desperate Housewives,* and *One Tree Hill* all seem pretty convincing in their dramatic sexcapades, with inappropriate camera angles and seductive body movements. Honestly, I don't care how old you are, no one benefits from these images.

If you think that I am overreacting, here's why: we are desensitized to how sexually saturated our culture has become. If you think that we should just ignore it, here's the thing: most of us aren't good at ignoring "it." In fact, in a moment of honesty, we would probably admit that we blend right in with the culture, and "it" plays a big role. We've learned that women are supposed to seduce men, and that it's even more of an accomplishment if the guy is in another relationship. That women should wear clothing that reveals their "assets." That we solve relationship problems by spicing things up. That we are to act nonchalant if the guy doesn't want to commit to a monogamous relationship. That sex is a means to an end. That successful women are aggressive, controlling, and erotic.

Even teen magazines offer advice for everything from giving great oral sex to knowing when you are ready for sex. Will anyone be honest with us about what sex is really like?

What We're Taught at Home

In the eighth grade, I heard some sketchy information about girls getting a "period" every month. *Why didn't I know about this before?* It was such a weird thing. Seven days later I didn't really know what was happening; I thought I had a diarrhea accident or something. When I described my symptoms to my mom, she explained that it was probably because I had started my menstrual cycle.

My family definitely didn't talk about sex; the topic grossed me out. When I was sixteen, I had one abstinence conversation with my family. In most families "the talk" consists of, "Don't have sex."

That, and "Dad will get the shotgun if a guy even thinks about asking you out." That's about it.

We didn't really talk about the benefits of waiting or how we should live out our abstinence commitments.

What We're Taught in Church

Many church groups simply don't talk to teens about sex. If churches discuss sex and relationships at all, the focus is on modesty for girls and self-control for boys. Speeches always end with "Don't have sex!" and a purity pledge. If high school and college age church groups do talk about sex and relationships, the sermon comes about once a year. For today's teen and young woman, these yearly messages are not enough to combat what they hear *daily* from everyone else.

Girls today want more information than previous generations because they live in a hypersexualized culture that gives them access to anything. So why are youth leaders still avoiding the sex topic by saying things like, "Guys are like the buzzing bees (horny) that want to go from flower to flower (girls) and pollinate (sex)"? After giving sad, pitiful explanations of sex, they think they delivered a good sex talk. What are they thinking? Young men *and* young women need to know that they will be sexually aroused, why they should demonstrate self-control, and how to succeed when they are sexually tempted. We can hear only so many "Don't have sex" messages without wanting to tune out the speaker. We need to hear more than the rules about sex. We need a little bit of motivation from time to time.

Some church women who "encourage" me to continue in my abstinence have good intentions, but their delivery is terrible. They don't act romantic or loving toward their husbands, don't seem as if they were ever in love, and don't seem like they even enjoy being married. If I talk about being in love with a guy, they just roll their eyes as if love is silly. It's tempting to think, *Why should I wait until*

I marry to have sex if no one who is married enjoys their spouse? That can't make for a great sex life. Young women need to know the consequences of having sex outside of marriage, but we also need to know the *benefits* of having sex *in* marriage. We need to know the truth about why people have sex and what happens during sex and sexual activity.

The Sex Talk

I guess you could say I had selective hearing. When certain people—like my sex-ed teachers and girls who slept around—tried to talk to me about sex and their sexual experiences, I didn't listen. The way they described sex, it sounded dirty, and I knew it was wrong to have sex unless I was married. So, though I grew up knowing absolutely nothing about sex, there came a point—at age twenty—when I started wondering what the fuss was about. I knew I could look in any bathroom stall or magazine to learn the "10 Ways to Make Him Cry During Sex," and I am sure that information is *very* interesting, but I wanted to know how to biblically feed my curiosity about sex. I was hesitant to explore this topic on my own because I didn't want to be corrupted by images and information that would cause me to stumble. I am sure that there are some aspects of sex that I just don't need to know right now. I realized that I had missed out on an actual "sex" talk with my mom, and suddenly I was very ready to talk.

I wasn't interested in what girls did with college boys. Alcohol factors into many girls' first sexual experience, and 85 percent of teenagers decide to have sex because their partner wants to.[1] I didn't want to hear sex stories from the girls who got drunk at a party and had sex with their boyfriend because he wanted it. *Loving* and *romantic* were not the words that came to mind as I listened to my friend describe how her boyfriend didn't want to wait for her to get comfortable before having sex, so she lay on a cold cement basement floor and pretended to enjoy it. She didn't really want to have sex, but thought she had to in order to keep her boyfriend. The sex was a scarring, emotional blur and when it was over they rejoined the party like nothing had happened. *Something had definitely happened!* Because the sexual experience was so emotionally confusing, in her future sexual experiences she tried to detach her feelings and pretend that sex was no big deal. Sex was no longer as special as she once thought it should be. Sex had been reduced to just something to do with a guy.

I wanted to know what sex was like in a loving, caring marriage relationship. I wanted to know what it was like to have sex without feeling dirty or having regrets. Call me a hopeless romantic, but I want sex to be something that I love to remember, not something I try to forget.

One night during my sophomore year in college while hanging out with my Christian girlfriends, our conversation moved to the subject of sex. This was a first for us. It seemed like a safe environment for me to ask a question that was really confusing to me, so I did. I moved a lot in school and I went to Christian schools during my latter years in grade school. Now, I understood anatomy, but I didn't really understand anything about the male and female bodies, like what happens before and after sex. I didn't really get the whole sex thing. So I asked my question, and at first my friends thought I was joking. Then their jaws dropped and some of them started to laugh when they realized that I was honestly confused. They explained what I'm sure they learned in the fifth grade—a guy's penis gets hard in order to have sex with a woman. *I didn't know that.* Then I had a million more questions.

So my senior year in college, I did the only logical thing I could think of: I planned a slumber party with my roommates . . . and my mom . . . to talk about sex. My poor mom, she was such a good sport that night. She invited her friend over so they could answer our questions as a team. I don't blame my mom for not wanting to be alone in a room with four girls asking about the intimate details of sex. During our discussion, I realized that my roommates were curious about things that I hadn't even thought of. It was shocking. The four of us were virgins and ready to understand the benefits of a healthy sex life in marriage. We didn't want to be the virgin who walked into our honeymoon suite and puked when our husband said what he wanted to do. *You want to do what?* I learned a lot that night. Although I definitely had more questions about sex after our talk, it ended up being good for me.

So why don't more mothers talk with their daughters about sex—real sex, biblical sex? I know most girls are afraid to talk to *anyone* about sex, *especially* their mom. Ninety-five percent of girls surveyed said they never discuss sexual subjects with their mom.[2] We either think that sex is "no big deal" or we worry about what our mom will think of our curiosity. *If I ask my mom a couple of sex questions, she will either assume I'm having sex and make me go on the pill, or ground me for life. At this rate, I won't be able to date until I'm thirty.* Most girls don't want to risk it, so they look to their friends and media to provide them with the needed answers. However, studies show that teenagers are less likely to start having sex when their mothers are involved in their lives and have a close relationship with them.[3]

In eighteenth-century England, women viewed sex in marriage as their duty, not to their husband, but to their government. Women were taught not to *enjoy* sex, but to *endure* it for the noble cause of having boys who would grow up and fight in the Queen's army.[4] That is rigidity at its peak! I can hear a daughter having the "sex talk" with her mom: "Mom, can I talk to you about sex with my future husband? I am really excited for sex and—" Her mom would interrupt her, "Ladies do not enjoy sex and we definitely don't talk about it. End of discussion."

I'm convinced that a lot of girls think the "sex talk" with their mom would go the same way today. Young women feel like it's taboo to talk honestly about sex. After all, "good girls don't talk like that," even if it is with our mothers. In today's society, talking about sex is forbidden, but engaging in sex . . . well, everyone's doing it. So let me get this straight, *talking* about sex is bad, but if you actually *have* sex it's okay? What a weird message to send women. When our parents are silent on this issue, we are forced to decide for ourselves.

Instead of being forced into making uninformed or bad decisions, let's just talk. Let's ask the questions we want to ask and get real answers from our moms, aunts, and female mentors instead of friends who lost their virginity in a basement. Choose wisely who you talk to about this subject. If your mom is not a Christian, isn't faithful to her husband, or is telling you to have sex and move in with your boyfriend, I suggest you talk to someone who will encourage you to wait to have sex until marriage. You are likely to receive a skewed, lustful, and emotionally detached view of sex if you talk to women who don't have a biblical view of sex.

Whatever your situation, you can find a trustworthy, godly female adult who will lovingly help answer some of your questions from a biblical viewpoint. Don't be embarrassed to ask questions. Remember, it wasn't until I was twenty that I actually understood how sex works. Your mom is probably just as nervous as you are about talking about sex, so work through it together. Oh, and don't forget to have ice cream and chocolate at the party; they make everyone feel a little more relaxed! To help get your conversation started, I've given you some questions that we asked my mom when we had the greatest slumber party ever! Even if you think you have it all figured out, try talking to your mom or your mentor anyway.

When asking these questions, remember that you don't need to know everything right now, and you can always have another "sex talk" before you get married.

- Do you and Dad still have sex?
- Is it always romantic to have sex?
- What does sex feel like?
- How long does sex last?
- Do you like sex every time you have it?
- How do you feel after sex? (Tired, close to Dad, excited, etc.)
- How often do you have sex?
- Do you like oral sex?
- What do you do during foreplay?
- Are there certain positions of sex that feel better or are more fun?
- How many times can you have sex in one day?
- How do you deal with your insecurities and being naked?
- Do you still have sex when you don't feel pretty, are sweaty or smelly, have bad breath, etc.?
- Do you have the lights on or off when you have sex?
- Do you always have sex in the same place?
- How do you clean yourself before you have sex?
- Why do some people scream when they have sex?
- I heard sex hurts the first few times. Does it always hurt?
- Why do people use lubrication?
- Is it true that guys get tired after sex?
- Why do some people get bladder infections after they have sex?
- How old can you get before you can't have sex anymore?
- Why do you think it's best to save sex until marriage?

Even after hearing answers to these questions, you may still have questions about sex. Most of us know that the Bible says to save sex for marriage, but is that *all* that the Bible says about sex? What does God, the Creator of the universe, have to say about sex and the sexes?

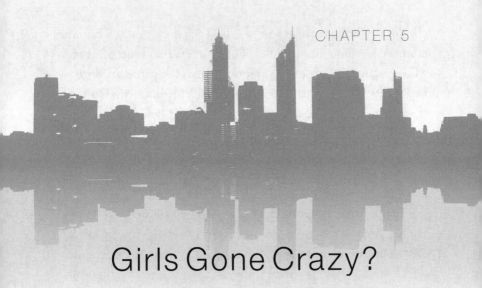

CHAPTER 5

Girls Gone Crazy?

Or, Is Thirty Years Too Long to Wait for Anything?

IF YOUR CHURCH IS ANYTHING LIKE MINE, single ladies lurk in parking lots, foyers, and sanctuaries. Like lions searching for prey, they wait for the next single guy to come along. As soon as they spot him, it's an all-out attack. Women run from all directions, plowing over kids and greeters, just to sit in his row. If he goes forward for prayer, you better believe at least five women will "lay on hands" with great concern for his "spiritual needs."

A couple of years ago, my friend and I went to a Christian conference and listened attentively as a young, Christian bachelor spoke with clarity and comedy. Afterward, women mobbed him, insisting that he sign their books, fliers, and shirts. By the look on his face, it was clear he thought some of their requests were a little odd (or maybe he thought some of the women were odd). From the moment he spoke until he flew home, he had a group of women who surrounded him more voraciously than the paparazzi do Britney Spears. This is when I found myself in a predicament: Do I join the swarm of girls who are drooling all over him (which is not something I do—there are enough groupies in the world already), do I lay low and catch his eye as he walks by (and pray he wants to talk to someone who isn't starstruck), or do I just ignore him (because how many people actually end up with a guy like him)?

Call me old-fashioned, but I want a guy to ask me out—to pursue me, not the other way around. I don't think it's a woman's job to ask out her dates. If a man wants to lead in the marriage relationship, he should start practicing *before* he's reciting his wedding vows. I have no desire to compete with seven other women for one guy's attention. If I did, I would go on *The Bachelor*. So what's a girl to do? Should we mob guys, ask them out, ignore them, or keep waiting for them to notice us?

The Bible says in Proverbs 18:22 that "He who finds a wife finds a good thing"; so why haven't I been "found" yet? I am fun, athletic, healthy, smart, responsible, friendly, happy, loving, and basically free of debt (my only debt is my car payment). I want to grow closer to God daily and eventually raise a family to do the same. I don't play games with guys and I don't lie—what you see is what you get. I want to be treated with love and respect, adoration, and compassion. I want to be spiritually, physically, emotionally, relationally, and mentally attracted to a man. I want to admire him and his walk with God. I want a man who is strong, funny, and sensitive, has a good work ethic, is an encourager and a servant, and passionately loves God. Is this too much to ask? Most people say it is, or they make up reasons why women my age are still single.

I have heard every reason why I and so many women my age are still single, and the explanations I hear are ridiculous. I know I am not perfect, and like everyone else, I am still a work in progress, but if you are trying to give me advice about my singleness, at least say something that makes sense. Of all the lame reasons I have heard so far, these are my favorites: "Your standards are too high," "You're too intimidating," "It's only when you least expect it that you will meet your future husband," "There must be something wrong with you," and last but not least, "God must want you to be single right now" or "Maybe God doesn't want you to get married."

Your Standards Are Too High

You have probably been told by a well-meaning parent, grandparent, or friend, "Your standards are too high, and if you don't lower them, you will never get married!" Exactly which standards should we lower, and at what cost? Why are my standards too high now when they weren't in high school or college? Do they want me to just get married, or get married to the right person and be happy and in love with him for the rest of my life? I have had a few offers of marriage. More on this later. Each guy had great qualities, just none I wanted to live with for the rest of my life. My standards are not too high.

I would argue that men justify their crude, licentious, and lackadaisical behaviors because women have *lowered* their standards, not *raised* them. In hopes of winning over a guy, women have tolerated and approved of ungentlemanly behavior. They have accepted and even encouraged men to continue acting like boys by believing and repeating stupid clichés like "Boys will be boys." I am convinced that these clichés were originally spoken by women who were embarrassed by a man's behavior, not proud of it.

All of my "high standards" can be summarized into three different categories: spiritual compatibility, friendship, and physical attraction. I want to share my spiritual growth with my husband, I want my husband to be my best friend, and you know I have to think he's fine! That is *not* too much to ask. I believe that in order to have a healthy, godly marriage, all of these requirements must be met. If the guy you're dating is not spiritually compatible, your friend, or someone you find attractive, get another man.

SPIRITUAL COMPATIBILITY

I am not going to go out with non-Christian men. I will not lower this standard. Even though it seems that non-Christian men are the only ones who have enough courage to ask me out, I don't go there. My junior year in college, a basketball player with an inflated ego decided that there was no risk in asking me out in front of seven of his teammates. He was completely shocked when I said, "Thank you for the compliment of asking me out, but no, I will not go out with you." I thought it was a kind yet firm way to say no. I thought he would drop it and move on, but I wasn't so fortunate.

Instead of walking away, he asked me more questions. "Lindsey, why won't you go out with me? I want to know."

This is new, I thought. I had never been asked *why* I wouldn't go out with someone. In the past when I declined a date invitation, the guy usually just said, "Okay," and moved on. I thought for a second and decided to tell him the truth. I was convinced that he could handle it.

"Well, Scott, let's just say that we want different things from a relationship. You will want to do things that I won't do."

"Like what?"

"For starters, I am not going to have sex until I get married. I know you, and I know this would be a problem for you."

"Lindsey, what are you talking about? I am only asking you to go on a date with me."

"And Scott, I am a Christian, and as far as I know, you are not. If we don't have our faiths in common, nothing else matters to me."

Throughout our dialogue I was praying that God would give me the words to say to this guy. I wanted to be kind yet strong so he and all the guys—who were definitely eavesdropping on our conversation—knew that I was a woman who would not compromise my standards for anyone.

"Lindsey, would you calm down? I just want to take you on a date. Let's go to dinner and maybe a movie. I am not asking you to have sex with me. I am not asking you to marry me. I just want to go on a date."

"Scott, you may not be asking for sex right this minute, but you will in the immediate future and you won't get it. Thank you for the compliment of asking me out, but the answer is still no."

When I told one of my friends what had happened, she urged me to reconsider and go out with Scott. She wouldn't dream of telling a college athlete no.

The following week I ran into Scott as he was bragging to the other basketball players about how he hooked up with some girl that weekend. He had sex with her and he couldn't even remember her name. I was really, really glad that God gave me the strength to stand up for my convictions. God really protected me from being corrupted by a guy who asked me out having only one thing on his mind.

FRIENDSHIP

Since I was in my mother's womb (or at least since I was really young), the need to date a good Christian boy was drilled into my head. In junior high I was taught the importance of being friends with a potential dater, which seemed like an impossible task. Seriously, have you ever tried to be friends with a guy who is in junior high? I am convinced that if junior high doesn't kill a girl, nothing will. Until recently I thought this whole "be friends with guys" thing was my mom's premeditated sabotage for my dating life. Surely it was her attempt to keep me single forever!

I won't say that I have it all figured out—I am still trying to understand what it looks like to be friends with the opposite sex—but I do know that you have to enjoy being friends with the guy you date.

You have to connect on a deeper level. He should be someone you want to talk to when you wake up and before going to bed. He should be the first person you want to call when you get a raise, your dog dies, or when you watch a good movie and wish you could have shared it with someone. You should be the kind of friends that are loyal, honest, trustworthy, and want what is best for the other person.

If you don't trust a guy enough to share your hopes, dreams, and struggles with him, then you shouldn't date him. Don't lower your standards to date someone who offers unwise advice or who you fight with every time you're together. Marriage is for life. If you can't be around him for a few hours without getting annoyed, don't think that it will be anything less than hell on earth to marry him and live in the same house together until you die. Not a good idea!

As it is vital to date a fellow believer, so too it is valuable to be his friend. But one crucial dating component is missing from this equation, and that is the need for physical attraction.

PHYSICAL ATTRACTION

Several Christian women have told me that physical attraction is not necessary in a romantic relationship. *What? Are you crazy?* They continued to say that even if I'm not attracted to a guy *now*, it doesn't mean I *couldn't* become attracted to him after getting to know him better. I believe that when you are initially attracted to a guy, get to know him better, and grow the list of reasons why you adore him, then he becomes *more* attractive to you, not attractive for the first time! You don't go from being repulsed by someone's looks on Monday to picturing having his kids on Friday. It doesn't work that way.

Girls are encouraged to date guys without being physically attracted to them, but are guys told the same thing? *Heck no!* I don't know any guy who would ask out a girl he's not attracted to. It's simple: if she's cute and nice, a guy will ask her out, but if she's only got a "great personality," he will not ask her out. Guys have better things to do with their time and money than to woo a girl they're not attracted to. Guys get this, so what is taking us women so long to figure it out?

I spent years trying to make myself attracted to "good, godly guys," but when the chemistry wasn't there, it wasn't there. I think one of the greatest mysteries in the world is what makes two people attracted to each other. I don't base everything on looks, but I don't think the "hottie" factor should be ignored either.

A few years ago I attended a Valentine's Day panel discussion at my church. Romance was the panel's theme, and the discussion centered on the panelists' views of romance and what they look for in the opposite sex. The panelists included a few singles in their early twenties and a married couple who was in their thirties. I was really excited to hear the women's responses when they were asked, "What do you look for in a guy?" However, after hearing a few women speak I was about to scream. As the panelists responded to this question, not one of them mentioned being physically attracted to the guy.

Finally they handed the microphone to the last single woman and she said something like, "It's really important to me that he eats healthy, exercises, and is athletic and in great shape." I was so encouraged, I wanted to jump out of my seat, but she continued talking. It was as if she thought to herself, *Oh my gosh, I can't believe you just said that to a room full of single men. You'd better do something quick or you will never get asked out.* So when she continued speaking it sounded nothing like her first sentence, "Well, actually, he doesn't have to be athletic. If he likes to *watch* sports, that works too. I don't have a certain 'type,' so if he is bald or overweight, that's okay." *What the heck, woman? You went from saying "athletic and in great shape" to talking about an average couch potato.* The next woman to speak was the married woman. She told the audience the truth—you have to be physically attracted to the guy.

Call me "rebellious," call me "worldly," call me whatever you want, but I am no longer compromising on physical attraction. If I am asked out by a guy and I can't picture myself wanting to kiss him, or at least hold his hand, then I know we are going to remain "just friends." My standards are not too high for wanting to date a guy that I'm attracted to. After all, I hope that my husband and I will have a lot of sex, and I don't know about you, but I don't want to think about having sex with "The Beast" (or someone I am not attracted to). Just thinking about that makes me queasy. I am not going to feel guilty anymore. I am not going to date some-one because I think I *should* be attracted to him. Being physically attracted to your man is a *must*.

My standards are not too high. However, if your standards are that he must be six-foot-two, have 210 pounds of muscular perfec-tion, dark brown hair, look like an Armani model, be a professional athlete, drive a Range Rover, want to have exactly four kids, and (after he's finished his career as an athlete) plan to work full time in the mission field for the rest of your married lives, then your stan-dards are too high. Instead of focusing on the particulars of your attraction to him, just make sure you hit the top three components of spiritual compatibility, friendship, and physical attraction. Let God surprise you with the rest of the details.

You Are Too Intimidating

Married couples and peers have suggested that I am still single because I intimidate guys. They say, "Guys are more insecure than you'd think, so when a pretty girl like you is smart and loves the Lord, guys don't feel comfortable asking you out. They don't think they will be good enough for you." Although their words are flattering, their explanation doesn't solve my problem: I am single and want to be married. When I see that a guy is shy, I initiate a "hello." I am a nice, outgoing person and I don't mind initiating a conversation to help him be less shy. If he can't go from there, why should it be my problem that he's afraid to talk to a pretty girl? Be a man, get some guts, and talk to me already! I won't bite. Women say it is hard to get a guy to say "I do," but it is especially hard if you can't even get him to say "hi."

Recently my mom and I needed help moving furniture. Since my mom is forever trying to be a successful matchmaker, she called our pastor and asked him to recruit a couple of single guys *my age* to help. The two guys showed up at our house around dinnertime, and because I thought they were staying for dinner, I spent the majority of the time manning the grill. It wasn't until I brought in the platters of food that I found out they weren't staying for a meal. Had I known this, I wouldn't have made so much food, nor would I have spent so much time outside grilling by myself.

When they left, my mom mentioned that I could have been more hospitable. Well, what she really said was, "Lindsey, Jake was really cute and you barely said hello to him. Now he probably thinks you aren't interested." (Leave it to moms to say something like this.) I didn't want Jake to feel like I wasn't interested, so when I saw him at church that Sunday I apologized for my preoccupation with the grill. I then said, "If you guys ever want to come over for dinner another time, we would love to thank you for helping us." I wasn't asking him out on a date, I just wanted to thank him and his friend for helping us. A strange thing happened at this point in our conversation. As I told him we would like to thank him for his help, midsentence he turned and walked away. *What the heck? You don't just walk away and ignore a girl who is inviting you over for dinner.*

You thank her for the offer, or at the very least, act like you heard her talking. What is with guys? I looked at my mom, who saw what happened from across the room, and we both started laughing. Maybe my friends are right. Maybe I do intimidate guys. Go figure.

He'll Come When You Least Expect It

I will probably puke if I hear one more person tell me something idiotic like, "It's when you least expect it that your future husband will come along." *Puhhlease.* I have been "least expecting it" for over thirty years now; any other suggestions? I have not put my life on hold for a man. I don't view marriage as the fairy-tale ending of life, like movies told me growing up. I have goals and a purpose to fulfill, with or without a husband. So explain to me how not thinking, not hoping, and not being excited about something makes that event come sooner? When I found out that my family was going to Disney World, I was so excited about going that I could hardly stand it. I thought about Disney World off and on from the time we made the reservations until the day we actually went. But whether I thought about Disney World or not, it didn't make the time go any faster. Each day still contains twenty-four hours, despite my thoughts or non-thoughts about what the future may hold.

In Scripture, God tells us to make plans while trusting Him for his timing and provision, so why is it considered taboo if one is "expectant" for marriage?[1] I am talking about normal women with a normal desire to get married, not an atypical "girl gone psycho" who buys her wedding gown before she even has a boyfriend. A woman hoping for marriage can prepare for married life in various ways that are clearly displayed in Proverbs 31. Just as with any new habit, lifestyle change, or spiritual discipline, developing godly attributes doesn't come naturally and—speaking from personal experience— requires a *lot* of practice. So, while I am single, I can prepare for marriage by practicing being selfless, responsible with money, generous, and compassionate. Ladies, no respectable guy wants to date or marry someone who is desperate, but it is okay to desire, expect, and prepare for marriage.

There Must Be Something Wrong with You

After a certain age, if you are an unmarried single woman, people turn on you. When I was in my teens and early twenties, people said, "Those guys must not know a good woman when they find one." Now that I am older, people have started to ask, "Why aren't you married yet?" as if I have done something wrong or have changed for the worse in the last five years. Sorry, but last I checked, I can't force guys to ask me out or talk to me. I can't create a magic love potion to make a smart, handsome, godly bachelor fall madly in love with me and propose. I am open to correction, I seek godly counsel, and trust me, my mentors and accountability partners do not hold back in letting me know when I need to work on something. So the next time someone (who doesn't even know me) hints that the reason I am not yet married is because of something I have done, they had better duck.

You're Supposed to Be Single

"Maybe God doesn't want you to get married." Why do so many people think this about older single women? God created, blessed, and sanctified marriage, yet people insist that I must be "called" to singleness simply because I haven't been asked by the right man. I fail to see how men taking their sweet time to mature, be responsible, and ask for a woman's hand in marriage somehow implies that *I* have missed my calling. The marrying age for women has continued to increase yearly since the 1960s.[2] More statistics show that the average marrying age for American women in 1950 was around twenty for women and twenty-three for men. In the late 1980s the average man married by the time he was twenty-six and the women by the age of twenty-four. And the trend continues.[3]

Our culture has changed—guys are no longer encouraged to grow up, assume responsibility, or marry. Amidst the Hollywood voices who exalt bachelorhood, there are very few individuals who are still encouraging guys to be men. Women are encouraged to attend college and pursue a career, thereby delaying the average age for marriage. So when did we start equating cultural shifts with God's desires for our lives? Just because our culture wants to redefine marriage and encourages people to delay "settling down" doesn't mean God's desire for men to marry women has changed.

In the New Testament, the apostle Paul exhorted singles to follow in his footsteps and live the single life to be more available to further the message of Christ.[4] His words have become the soapbox on which people stand as they try to convince us older single women that if we are not married by a certain age, then singleness must be our calling. However, I do not see this mandate in Scripture. I've heard of a few individuals who knew from a young age that God was calling them into a life of singleness. These people were excited about singleness and about devoting all of their time and talents toward missions and ministry. These individuals weren't strong-armed into the deal, they willingly volunteered for it.

Singleness is a good thing, it's a godly thing, it's beneficial in so many ways, but I truly believe that if God were calling me into singleness for the rest of my life, He would let me know. God directs me in every other area, so why wouldn't He direct me in this area? Do people think about the implications of what they say when they tell women, "Maybe God has called you to singleness"? They imply that we older single women must not be hearing from the Lord or we are disobeying God's calling on our lives by remaining hopeful for marriage. These implications are hurtful and frustrating.

Statements like "You must be single right now because God wants you to be single" make me question the speaker's view of God. Just because God has *allowed* something to take place in our lives doesn't mean that He initiated the circumstance. After all, humans do have free will, and this world is sinful. God uses difficult situations to mold us to be more like Him, but it doesn't mean that the situations (like singleness) were "meant to be" or are *blessed* by God. No one really knows why God allows certain things to happen (like singleness for the women who desire to be married), and yet, not one of our situations takes God by surprise.

Bouncing Back from Criticism

Regardless of the criticism I receive about my character—due to my protracted singleness—I try to use it to keep myself in check. Frequently I allow friends to help me evaluate my heart, attitude, motives, and actions. I think it's important to constantly make sure I am on the right track. As long as I am continually growing into the godly woman He wants me to be, I don't need to worry about other people's opinions about my singleness. I already know I am not perfect, but I am perfectly made. So what about you? Maybe you have experienced people telling you that your singleness is something that you have brought upon yourself, and maybe you have believed it. Or, maybe you think the problem lies with the men. Contrary to popular e-mails that circulate with sayings like, "All of women's problems start with men," I don't think that men are completely to blame for the plight of us older single women.

CHAPTER 6

Bringin' Sexy Back

WHERE ARE ALL THE SEXY, CHRISTIAN MEN? Young Christian guys have lost touch with what it means to really be sexy, and what's worse, we women have approved of it. Today's average Christian male is known for being lackadaisical in his faith, or "not serious about his walk right now." The modern-day Christian guy embraces God and His goodness, yet still wants to be a sexually stimulated club-hopper who arrives twenty minutes late to church, sits in the back row, falls asleep halfway through the sermon, and lives the life of bachelorhood well into his thirties.

Let me just start off by saying I love men. I really do. I am not some Femi-Nazi who thinks that men are the root cause of all of the problems in society. I don't think *all* guys are objectionable. I believe there are great guys out there . . . somewhere. Last I checked, the U.S. does not have a shortage of males, but we seem to have a shortage of men. Even worse is the sparcity of Christian men who are passionate about pursuing a relationship with God and accepting the God-given responsibilities of having a wife and children. Although we have statistics to prove it, we church-attending women don't need national surveys to remind us that women fill more seats in church on Sunday than do men.[1] The unbalanced numbers of men and women attending church have seriously affected the Christian dating scene. Because guys are in the minority in Christian settings, they have more women to choose from and are less eager to commit to just one. Nothing frustrates me more than single, godly guys who put off accepting their God-given roles as leaders in society and in the home. Grow up, be a godly man, and commit already!

Wanted: Men

As of February 2008, the U.S. population totaled around 303 million.[2] More than 230 million of those individuals were eighteen years or older. About 108 million attended church the week prior to taking the survey (a typical weekend—not including a special event such as a wedding or a funeral). Out of that group, 40.6 million of those individuals were men, and only 15.4 million were single.[3] These various polls and statistics estimate that there are 15.4 million men in the U.S. who are eighteen years or older, single, and attended church the week before the study. This small number of available men (compared to 41.9 million unmarried men in the general population[4]) gets smaller when you factor in their gender preference, age, spiritual maturity and beliefs, denominational preference, personality, individual interests, location, and whether they desire to marry. All this to say, I have yet to meet a Christian woman who complains about there being *too many* eligible Christian bachelors: we all know there are not enough.

Not only is there a shortage of Christian guys, but a shortage of Christian men who will actively pursue a relationship with a Christian woman. When we get asked out by guys, it's at places like the grocery store and ice cream shop, not at Christian events. Non-Christian guys ask me out in coffee shops and restaurants, while I am working, and once I was asked out at a stoplight as the guy tossed me a rose from his car. So what the heck is going on with Christian guys? Why aren't they taking the initiative in talking to women? Where are the men who will lead by serving and praying, and who will stand up for what is right? I am not talking about the counterfeits who go to church still hung over from the night before. I want to know where the godly, sexy, Christian men are.

In previous generations, guys weren't considered men until they married and started a family. Being a man was encouraged and promoted by his family and society as a whole. Our culture is trying to redefine what it means to be a man and woman. Many people believe that girls are no different than boys and all should be treated the same. Sorry, but guys and girls *are* different on so many levels.[5] We don't need more men to be like women, or women who will act like men.

A Missing Link

A lot of us didn't grow up with both of our biological parents and we've never seen what a sexy, godly man looks like. We have no idea how that kind of man acts and treats women. We think we're doing fine in our choices of men, but that's only because we don't have anyone better to compare them to. On the other side, because so many guys didn't grow up learning what it looks like to be a real man, they don't know how to treat women. Instead of honoring and blessing women, they neglect, abuse, and ignore women. Bottom line: guys don't know how to be sexy, godly men, and women don't know how to tell the difference.

I don't know what it was like growing up in your home, but my parents divorced when I was nine. After their divorce I had a hard time trusting men, so I kept my distance from them. Throughout high school and college I wanted to believe that I would get married someday, but because I saw so many marriages fail, I wasn't convinced that marriage could last a lifetime. I was almost scared away from marriage forever.

After my parents divorced, my mom's friends would often come over and talk about life, love, and relationships. When I asked my mom's divorced friends why they thought their marriages failed, many said, "We just didn't know each other well enough." One woman's story began in college. She attended an out-of-state college, and when she came home for break, she worked in a local restaurant to pay for her tuition. At the restaurant, she met her future husband. They dated while she was home for summer break, then switched to a long-distance relationship during her last semester of school. During the occasions they talked and spent time together, he seemed like he was really *interested* in God, like he really *loved* God. She was so excited about their similarities that the relationship continued despite the distance. That summer they spent two months together and the next time they saw each other they got engaged. After the first year of marriage, he stopped praying with her, didn't attend church with her anymore, and was completely indifferent about his faith. He eventually committed adultery, and they divorced after being married for eleven years.

This story stuck with me for so many years as I wrestled with my own fears of marrying someone like that. I thought, *What if I can't tell if he's really serious about God?* My fears were validated over and over in my dating relationships when guys told me they were Christians but then didn't act like it.

Waiting for My Prince Charming

Through the process of waiting for my "Prince Charming" to come and sweep me off my feet, I have observed fewer and fewer men like the valiant ones described in previous generations, and more and more like the prince from *Shrek 2*. Fewer than a hundred years ago, men were chastised for not taking on the responsibility of a wife and family at a young age.[6] Today Hugh Hefner, an eighty-three-year-old bachelor king in the porn industry, is praised for his promiscuous lifestyle. In contrast, my grandparents were married by the time they were nineteen years old and were married for fifty plus years until my grandpa passed away. Today, the average nineteen-year-old male is too busy playing Wii to show up to work on time, let alone take on the responsibilities of a family.

So what's changed? Well, for starters, guys are not being encouraged and trained to be responsible husbands. As men have fun living free of any responsibilities, the average marrying age increases yearly. Gradual shifts in the accepted cultural ideologies have had disastrous effects on marriage. Factors such as the feminist movement, "free sex" movement in the sixties, homosexual practices, divorce rates, and protracted adolescence have all contributed to the increasing numbers of older single women and grown guys who behave like fraternity brothers. What our society needs is fewer guys who are unmotivated, noncommittal, and addicted to video games, and more men who are dedicated to becoming Christian leaders.

I had a "boyfriend" in junior high for about a week, and unfortunately we kissed once. During that kiss he kept trying to unbutton my shirt, so I kicked him out of my house. In high school I dated a guy who wasn't interested in me after I told him my sexual boundaries. I said no to the majority of guys in college who asked me out. I wasn't interested in dating guys who got high every day, cheated on their tests, and slept with every girl they dated (and many they didn't date). These guys had no goals or future ambitions beyond the four parties they were invited to that weekend, and their idea of romance was trying to bribe me to write their papers for them.

During my senior year in college, I dated the man who I thought I was going to marry. He was amazing, handsome, and I was convinced that he was committed to loving and obeying God. We met in college and were friends for five years before we dated, but our romantic relationship started *after* he graduated and moved over three thousand miles away. After dating long distance for six months, he was supposed to fly to Colorado for my college graduation, but instead of calling to say he was at the airport, he called and said he was having nightmares about us. It was a combination of the nightmares and his feeling that he didn't need to pursue me anymore that convinced him to stay home. After he told me this he said, "But I don't think our relationship needs to change." *He didn't think this would change our relationship?* Six months earlier he said he was pursuing me with the intentions of marrying me. However, these were not his intentions now, so I insisted that we break up.

Less than a month after our breakup he started dating another woman. A few more months passed and he called to tell me he was engaged. Another month passed and he asked me to spend the week with him while he was in town on a business trip. I thought it was a bad idea to meet with him without his fiancée, so I didn't visit him. When I didn't hear from him for almost a year, I figured we would never talk again and that was good for me. After all, what wife wants her husband spending time with his hot ex-girlfriend? When I came home from work one day my roommate said, "You will never guess who called you today." To my astonishment it was my ex. He told my roommate that after being married for a month he realized that marriage was not what he thought it would be. He said it was really hard. *How can marriage be hard after being married for a month? Seriously. The honeymoon takes one or two weeks, and when you get home, you open all the fun gifts you received from the wedding. How horrible can that be?*

I thought it was strange to hear from him after such a long time. I didn't know what to do, or why he called, so I decided to avoid the drama by ignoring his call. When he called me again the next day, I decided to see what he wanted. Little did I know the conversation would go from weird to worse. After being married for less than a month, he confessed, "I think I should get a divorce. I should have married you." *I thought this guy was godly and selfless, and now he tells me that he wants to divorce his wife and marry me? Was he always like this or has he changed since we broke up? If he was like this when we dated, how did I not see it?*

While I recoiled from this news, he continued to tell me how he thought about me every day and wondered if I ever thought about him. He said he dreamt about me almost every night and he missed me. Instead of giving him hope of a future between us, I gave him a lecture. What kind of guy calls his ex after being married for a month and says he married the wrong woman? I couldn't believe this guy. As a Christian, divorce should not be an option. Before I had the chance to process what he was saying, I realized that he probably would have said the same thing about any woman he married, even me. I don't know what compelled him to act this way. For the sake of his wife and marriage, I hope it was just a momentary lapse in his judgment, because this is not the way God wants men to live.

This conversation made me both confused and relieved. I was confused about how to discern a man's heart in my future dating relationships. I did *not* want to repeat this scenario. I was sad to learn that he was not the person I thought he was, but I was *so relieved* that I didn't marry him! After retelling this conversation to my accountability partner, we praised God for blessing me and protecting me. Even though I was sad and confused when our relationship ended, I thank God that we broke up.

Counterfeit Men

The high school I attended had more than three thousand students. There were a handful of cute guys, but only a few were Christians. My college had around thirty thousand students and thousands of cute guys. So many men, but so little time. At first, I was excited to meet new guys! That is, until I had conversations with them. *Why do guys try to impress girls by telling us how many parties they got drunk at last week?* There were a few "hotties" in the campus Christian groups, but many of them turned out to be posers. Their idea of living for God was either wearing a WWJD bracelet while they got drunk, or dating both me *and* my roommate. Regardless of where I have lived, worked, or played, my "Prince Charming" seems to be lost or stuck in a Cinderella movie. Enough is enough—it's time for all the sexy Christian men to come out of hiding! But how can we spot sexy Christian men amid all the counterfeits?

"THE KING OF SEX"

It's easy to conclude that counterfeit men are those in the Hollywood scene, but many of them can be found sitting next to you in the pew on Sunday. These counterfeits place guys like Justin Timberlake as their role model. In 2006, *Rolling Stone* named Justin Timberlake the "King of Sex" as they promoted his Future Sex/Love tour.[7] But everything—from his lyrics to the dancing girls in his music videos to the horrible halftime show where he ripped off Janet Jackson's top and exposed her breast—tells me that Justin wouldn't know sexy if it hit him in the face. From a woman's perspective, there is nothing sexy about a guy who surrounds himself with dancing girls in lingerie, supermodels, and actresses. Boosting his sales by using these women as sex symbols and degrading their value as women is not sexy. For all the JT fans out there, sorry, Justin's actions don't support his "sexy" claims. No woman should have to give sex or compete with other women sexually to earn a guy's admiration. A former member of the boy band 'N Sync, JT may have looks that some women like—he's got talent for sure—but without Christ he is about as opposite of sexy as it gets. Regardless of what he titles his next tour, and despite *Rolling Stone's* claims that he is the "King of Sex," he is *not* sexy. He's got a long journey ahead of him until he can *really* be sexy.

EXPOSED!

Counterfeit Christian men do and say whatever it takes to win a girl over. These guys are experts at talking "Christianese" but have no idea what it really means to live a life submitted to God. Counterfeits selfishly take from relationships and give nothing but heartbreak in return. They act as if it's a chore to be polite and courteous, and get annoyed when a woman suggests they open her car door or pay for their date. They are looking for a sugar mamma and demand sexual favors before they commit to a relationship. To make matters worse, when the Counterfeits decide to pursue a woman, their leadership lacks integrity and holiness. These jokers say things like, "I go to church. I pray. I could see myself marrying someone like you." However, when you get to know them better, you find out what they really think about you when they say things like, "You're just not sexual enough with me." *Are you serious?* Counterfeits masquerade as godly men but are exposed by their inconsistencies between true faith and their words and actions. Get rid of them and date a real man. The real men, the sexy men, the alluring men are those whose lives emanate the love and appeal that can only come from a personal relationship with Christ.

Sexy Men

I expect the men I date to be sexy, strong, godly men. This should not be asking too much. The truth of the matter is we want the best man possible. Why not? We deserve nothing less than the best. We don't want an arrogant, lackadaisical guy who can't hold a steady job and still relies on his parents to pay his rent. We want a strong, intelligent, responsible, and respectable man. (It helps when he smells good too! What, I'm human aren't I? Have you ever been talking with your friends when out of the corner of your eye you see a man walk by and suddenly get a whiff of what heaven probably smells like? It doesn't matter what you were talking about, you just have to see if the guy looks as good as he smells.) Women are attracted to men who aren't socially awkward and can hold a conversation. Contrary to popular opinion, women don't want to be their boyfriend's "mother." Honestly, we just want them to have their stuff together and be confident. We have enough to do as it is. We don't need to add anything else to our to-do lists.

So what is the definition of a sexy man? Sexy men are excited about living like Jesus and attempt to submit to God in every area of their lives. Sexiness is found in selfless men who are humble and in touch with their thoughts and emotions; they love to learn and find joy in blessing others. Sexy men are those who treat *all* women with respect (not just the ones they are trying to date). They are faithful, romantic, hardworking, wise, and disciplined. These men are strong enough to stand up for what is right, but gentle enough to love a woman. Sexy men aren't embarrassed to sing worship songs aloud.

Sexiness is when a man does what he says, is committed to his family, and has his priorities in order. Sexy men are those who try to understand their girlfriend or wife and go to great lengths to express their love. Contrary to *People* magazine's annual "Top 25 Sexiest Men Alive" list, the sexiest men have more than great looks and big bank accounts. They are men whose lives demonstrate their integrity and godly character. They are spiritually maturing and responsible gentlemen. Sexy men are the ones who will take the time to listen, *really* listen. They love to hear your opinions, thoughts, hopes, fears, and insecurities, and want to help you accomplish your best.

Godly, sexy Christian men do not date a woman with the hopes of satisfying their sexual desires, but to romance her with the intentions of purity and marriage. Sexy men are those who realize that *you* are worth waiting for sexually. These men will exert great effort to keep a woman's mind, body, and soul sexually pure, and they will keep her away from any compromising or tempting situations.

And last but not least, sexy men are funny! They make you laugh, not at other people's flaws, but because they are just so dang cute.

Recently I went on a date with a guy and I laughed for a week afterward just thinking about how much fun we had together. When I think about funny guys, I think of my friend Nick T. He is especially sweet and funny. Nick loves God, but he doesn't take himself too seriously either—a killer combo for sure. I have no doubt that Nick reads his Bible often. However, just in case he misses a day, he nicknamed his bed "the word," so he could honestly tell girls that he was "in the word" (the Bible) every day! Is that funny or what?

It's easy to conclude that sexy, godly men either don't exist, are all married, or are over the age of sixty. After all, single guys our age aren't like this, right? Wrong. It *is* possible to meet a sexy, godly man, even at a young age. I crushed on at least four different Christian guys who I knew in high school, and in college I met awesome men who were part of a Christian fraternity.

Ladies, sexy men *do exist*. Although I can't always pinpoint their exact location, I have heard rumors about sexy men and have met a few along the way. Many of my friends have found some to marry, so don't lose hope just yet. One day a sexy, godly guy will come along and will ask you out. When that day finally comes, you need to be prepared. I have a simple, small word that helps me weed out Counterfeits and make room for sexy men. That word is *SPERM*. That's right. This five-letter word will help you evaluate a man. Simply based on a guy's SPERM, you'll learn how to determine if a guy is a keeper.

CHAPTER 7

Evaluating His SPERM Count

DO YOU EVER FEEL LIKE YOU are in a dating rut? Do you seem to always *fall* for the wrong kind of guy? Are you ready to date a guy who is completely different from your exes; a guy who is actually good for you? This chapter will help you realize who you are, what you really need from a healthy dating relationship, and how to recognize good, godly men when you meet them.

Sometimes we go from one bad relationship to another. We wonder why we keep *falling* for the wrong guys, but we don't take time to figure it out. To know why we fall for the wrong guys, we must first take a deep look at ourselves. Maybe we come from a broken home and don't know what a healthy relationship looks like. Maybe we didn't have a loving relationship with our father. Maybe we are insecure, don't know ourselves, lack maturity, don't know what to look for in guys, or have unrealistic expectations for relationships (like expecting men to fill the role that only God can).

In my observations, women take one of two roads when they lack a positive fatherly influence: they either keep their distance from men because they don't trust them, or they run to men in hopes of finding love and acceptance from them. Both extremes are harmful as we establish and maintain our identities as women and detrimental to our relationships with men. Unless we address our insecurities, create boundaries and expectations for the men we will date, ask God to heal us from the heartache caused by our absent fathers and jerky exes, and understand what love really is, we will continue to fall for the wrong guy. What we need is a klutz-proof relationship plan.

A Klutz-Proof Relationship Plan

People don't fall in love, they fall in holes. Falling, a habit of clumsy and unobservant people, is not an action that will help two people identify and sustain a healthy, committed relationship. Because if you can "fall in love," then you can "fall out of love," and the relationship ends as clumsily as it began. To keep from falling for the wrong guy, come up with a plan and stick to it!

Everyone has dating standards and expectations. Problems arise when our standards aren't high enough. Make sure your standards are high, and don't confuse biblical standards with what's portrayed in movies. Unfortunately, so many of us have compromised our standards for so long that we don't even know what to look for in a guy anymore, and we definitely don't know what it really takes to make a marriage last "until death do us part." Our lack of knowledge in these areas is evident when we add names of the wrong type of guys to our list of exes, stay with the wrong guys way too long, and jump right into another relationship before we even process what went wrong in the last one. Other times we go back to a guy even though he treats us poorly, simply because the relationship is comfortable, or because we're scared to be single. And ladies, let's just be honest—some of us jump into relationships without first taking time to know and evaluate the man we are "jumping" in with. And we wonder why we keep getting our heart broken.

For our outcome to change, our process needs to change, or we'll become stuck in an insane cycle of doing the same thing over and over again expecting a different result. It's time that we stop *falling* in love and start *growing* in love. To do this, we first need to analyze ourselves. Self-analysis is a process of evaluating our God-given likes, dislikes, needs, talents, and dreams. Only after we understand ourselves can we properly evaluate men and decide if we have enough common ground to move forward in a dating relationship.

If you don't take time to figure out your likes and dislikes, you might get guys to fall in love with you, but is it the *real* you? It is natural to want people to like us, but sometimes what also seems natural is to try to be someone we aren't. Remember that the real you is always better than the fake somebody else. Don't try to be someone you aren't—you have a better chance at impressing a guy by being yourself. *Why*, you ask, *do I need to know myself before I can be ready for a stable, romantic relationship?* Well, in order to love another person, you have to first love yourself. Love yourself enough to know who you are and what you are looking for in a future husband. It takes maturity and wisdom to evaluate your life and to reflect on where you have come from, where you are at, and where you are going. When you know these important things about yourself, you will have more confidence and clarity in knowing what you want as well as what you deserve.

After taking an honest look at yourself, get ready to evaluate the guys around you. In restaurants, watch how they treat the servers. Among family, friends, or strangers, watch how they handle differing opinions, fights, or annoying siblings. With close observation you will notice that each guy has a theme that describes his character. In order to conclude that a guy has the essential characteristics that make him a man, you have to first evaluate his SPERM count. I am not talking about actual *sperm*, although the word makes girls laugh. I am talking about the acronym *S-P-E-R-M*. This acronym represents the five main areas to evaluate as we observe men. SPERM stands for Spiritual, Physical, Emotional, Relational, Monetary.

<u>S</u>PERM: Spiritual

Guys who say they are Christians are rare, and men who actually act like it are extremely rare. On my quest to find a "good Christian man," I meet plenty of guys who say they were "raised Christian," "believe in a God," or "are spiritual." Their families went to church on the major holidays and had a Bible somewhere in the house. Until my sophomore year in high school, I thought that was good enough for me. *It wasn't.* It's not good enough to date a guy who is "interested" in my faith, or even one who will go to church with me. Unless we both prioritize loving and obeying God first, then we are not a good fit. Sure I might be able to witness to the guy for a little while, but slowly my witness goes out the window. It is so easy to compromise and forsake my values when I date guys who aren't committed Christians. Although most men will never admit it, they want a woman who won't compromise her values for anyone. Men respect women who stick up for themselves. The guys who pressured and teased me the most in high school and college were the same guys who later told me how much they admired me for sticking to my beliefs. (It is only when our actions match our words that others are convinced we really trust God.)

In evaluating a guy to see if he really is a godly man, look at where he is going and where he is leading others. Men are supposed to lead in the marriage relationship, right? So before you get into a relationship with a guy, figure out where he is going and if you would benefit from traveling on that same path. If he is a good man, the path that he will lead you on is the one that directs you to God.

The way he lives his life, the decisions he makes, and his relationship with God should inspire and challenge you to spend more time with God. When you find a man worth keeping, you will be motivated to deepen your relationship with the Creator.

If you are having a tough time figuring out the path a guy is on, ask trusted friends for their observations in addition to observing *your* relationship with God and *your* thought life, both when you are together and when you're apart. With the right man you will run *to* God with a desire to be closer to Him. But when you are with the wrong guy, you will distance yourself *from* God out of fear, guilt, and regret. The wrong guy will make you feel good when you are with him, but when you're away from him, you'll be in turmoil about the relationship. With a guy who is your spiritual equal, you *both* will be encouraged and refreshed in all areas of your life.

SP̲ERM: Physical

In evaluating a guy physically, make sure he has a six pack, chiseled torso, and tight buns! Ha! Just kidding. Although I am not completely devastated when I see a guy who has taken extra time to sculpt his muscles into perfect form, this is *not* what I mean. We need to evaluate what his physical boundaries and goals are. We evaluate this area as a way of protecting ourselves. We don't stand a chance of being sexually pure unless we first talk about boundaries with a guy. Last I checked, no one is invincible—every one of us is open to sexual temptation. If you flirt with sexual temptations and are sexually active, you will experience the negative consequences of your choices. Some of those consequences are harder to deal with than others, but regardless, all negative sexual consequences can be avoided if you and your guy define how you will live a sexually pure lifestyle. If and when you realize a guy's physical boundaries are more sexual than yours, I suggest that you run, don't walk, and get the heck out of there.

Unfortunately I dated a guy for a long time who disapproved of my boundaries. He said I wasn't "sexual enough" for him. I still don't understand how a guy who says he's a Christian can tell his girlfriend that she is not "sexual enough" for him. To this day I thank God for reminding me that I don't need to give myself sexually to a man to try and earn his approval or affection. Praise God for giving me the strength to stick up for myself and end that relationship. You too will probably hear something similar from a guy someday, and when you do, ask yourself why you think God wants you to continue to date him. Trust me, it is so much more enjoyable to wait to date a man who will respect your boundaries, your heart, and your body, than it is to be with someone and constantly feel like he is more interested in the size of your breasts versus the size of your heart. Don't be embarrassed to communicate your physical boundaries with your potential dater, don't be shy about asking his, and don't be afraid to run away when his standards aren't high enough for you.

I am sure that not everyone who reads this book is a virgin, but lost virginity should not be your focus. What you need to focus on is how valuable you are as a woman. You are so precious to God. He wants the best for you, really! I don't know what your physical boundaries and explorations have been up until today, but it is not too late to establish new boundaries. You may think "It's too late, I have gone too far," but please listen to what I am saying—it is *never* too late to change. Regardless of your past sexual involvement, the wrong kind of guys will date you in hopes of getting you to go even further sexually, but you can change this. You *can* reverse the sexual progression that has been associated with your reputation. You can redraw the line. Don't ever believe the lie that you have to give sexual favors to the next guy you date because you did that in your past.

My sexual boundary is kissing on the lips—I won't go any further—and honestly, most times kissing is too much for me. Guilt-free kissing for me looks like this: we don't make sensual kissing noises, lie down, kiss for more than thirty seconds, or let our minds think about sexual things. I don't know if you have ever tried to kiss a guy without breaking the above boundaries, but for me, it's hard. Since I have had a lot of practice with being a virgin, I have gotten really good at not giving in to my sexual cravings. As good and as trained as I might be, I am so weak. The slightest things tempt me, and I think if most of us are honest in this area, you probably fall into the same category as me. Even if I kiss my boyfriend and stay within the above boundaries, but my heart is not pure (i.e., if I am lusting or purposefully trying to get aroused or arouse my boyfriend) then at that moment, according to how the Bible defines purity, I have not kept myself pure.

Although I am not trying to convince you to wait until you are married to kiss a guy, I will say this: it is so freeing to go to bed at night and know that God is proud of you and the way you treated your boyfriend. Seriously, nothing feels as good as staying pure before God. Sometimes, when I think about the guys I kissed in the past, I feel nauseous. It seriously makes me want to upchuck my lunch . . . gross. I wish that I had never kissed them. There were so many times when I struggled to keep my thoughts pure, and when I was honest about my struggle, we didn't kiss until I was able to do so without lusting. Several times in past relationships, when my boyfriend dropped me off at home, I felt guilty because we had gone too far. I hated feeling like that, feeling like I let both God and myself down. I flirted with temptation and I let my sexual desires get the best of my thought life. I have kissed men in ways that were tempting to both of us. At times I was so aroused all I could think about was sex. I felt so much shame afterward. But it wasn't until I was honest with myself about my thoughts and sexual temptations that I drew the line at kissing (with the above restrictions).

Honesty has been one tool that has kept me sexually pure in my relationships. Be honest with your boyfriend about your thoughts and feelings when you are together. Recognize what gets you "excited" and establish plans to avoid the temptation altogether. Trust me, the right man for you is one who is honest about his struggles and seeks out a godly man to mentor him and hold him accountable for his thoughts, actions, and the images he looks at. If you are interested in a man who views pornographic materials, listens to sexually explicit music, and entertains crude sexual talk, he is not the man for you. He will not value you as the beautiful creation God made you to be. If a guy thinks that he is "strong enough" to "handle" his temptations, run away and get out of that relationship. Sin and temptation should not be things we "handle," but things we flee and avoid altogether. Only the prideful will convince themselves that they are strong enough to handle or endure temptation. The humble will admit when they are tempted and immediately remove themselves from the temptation. Make sure you find a guy who is honest about his temptations.

It's when couples fail to talk about boundaries or ignore differences in the other's boundaries that lines are crossed and lives are forever changed. One discussion about your boundaries can save you from having several discussions later with your families and friends. Avoid the drama—purposefully talk about your physical boundaries *before* committing to a relationship with a guy. Make sure you have similar spiritual beliefs and physical boundaries.

SPERM: Emotional

For some strange reason, God gave women periods, and the diverse emotions that accompany them. *That's a nice way of describing what we go through, huh?* I still don't understand why God allows our emotions to fluctuate when the chemicals change in our bodies, *but whatever.* Sometimes I think that God gave women periods as a way to "clear the air" in our relationships. Some women suppress their emotions and act as if things don't bother them, but when their period comes, get out of Dodge. The term *liquid courage* is used to describe someone who needs alcohol to express what he or she lacks the courage to say while sober. Similarly, our periods tend to evoke a hidden boldness which motivates us to discuss issues that we have kept bottled up. But regardless of one's gender, when someone does not control how and when he or she expresses emotions or is not in touch with their emotions at all, the end result is always hurt feelings and tons of drama. So the third area to evaluate in a guy is his emotional range and how he expresses his emotions.

One of the easiest ways to discern whether or not you should date a guy is by observing his emotions and emotional consistency. Save yourself the heartache of being in an emotionally unhealthy relationship by figuring out this area of his life before entertaining the thought of a relationship. Figure out his dominating emotions. When he plays sports, how does he act when he makes a bad play or when one of his teammates does? Does he express consistency in his attitudes and emotions with everyone, or does he behave differently when you are around? Does he make decisions based on how he feels or based on what God's Word says to do? Does he react immediately to something, or does he take time to process his thoughts and communicate with sensitivity, grace, and appropriate timing? What influences his emotions? If he loses a game, fails a test, or is reprimanded by his boss, how long does it take him to recover? What are his overall attitudes about life, love, friendships, and women? Is he kind or sarcastic? Is he sincere or arrogant? Does he even know he has feelings and does he allow you to express yours? A guy's emotions and the way he expresses them will directly affect the woman he is with, so don't overlook this area.

On an even more serious note, how does your guy act when he is mad? Is he quick to get upset, does he yell when he is mad, does he get mean when he doesn't get his way? Does he pound holes in the wall? Does he do things that could harm himself or others? Does he take his anger out on you? Many women have dated or are dating an abusive man, and there is no reason for it. No one deserves to be treated disrespectfully, and no one deserves to be harmed or threatened in a relationship. Please hear what I am saying, if you or someone you know is in a relationship with a guy who they are afraid of, please get help. There are so many free resources for women who need a safe place to get away from an abusive guy. And once you get out of an abusive relationship, get counseling and figure out *why* you are letting people treat you poorly. Don't date another guy until you are convinced that you deserve nothing but the best—the very best. Stop defending men who demoralize you, and start sticking up for yourself and the fact that you deserve to be treated with loving-kindness. Although at first you may be afraid of being alone, believe me when I say that you are stronger, smarter, and more loveable than you are probably giving yourself credit for.

SPE_RM: Relational

Have you ever been attracted to a guy who seemed sweet and romantic, only to find out later that it was all an act? Yes, your friends, your parents, and even your dog tried to warn you about how he was with other people and other women, but you just didn't listen. I know what you are thinking: "He isn't that way with me" and "You don't know him like I do." I have been that girl. Unfortunately, sometimes we don't believe the truth about a guy until it is too late. And many times we defend their actions because we are afraid of being alone.

In college I liked entering the gym's weight room in stealth mode so guys didn't know I was there right away. Many male athletes were nice to me; they flattered me and gave me a lot of attention. Maybe I had a problem trusting men, or maybe I was wise in wondering about the sincerity of these guys. Regardless, I had to find out if their walk was as big as their talk. I needed to know if they were the real deal or excellent actors. One day after stretching with my trainer I was walking to the ice bath and saw two football players getting in.

I had been on several dates with one of them and daily prayed for God to show me the kind of guy he really was. The ice tub was too small for the three of us, so I decided to wait in the training room until they were finished. Before they got in the tub I saw them talking about something, then they grabbed their towels and left the training room. *Sweet!* They must have decided to use one of the ice baths closer to the field instead. My trainer urged me to jump in before any other players came along, so I did.

After spending five minutes in the miserably cold water, I saw the same two guys returning. Once they saw me in the ice bath I could tell they were angry. They started yelling at me and swearing, so I doubt they heard me say, "Sorry, I didn't think you guys were coming back." They left cursing and putting me down. As they left I couldn't help but smile. I was smiling because I got the ice bath, which was an obvious victory, and because God showed me this guy's heart. Prior to this day, he had always been a gentleman around me and showered me with attention. He opened my doors, paid for our dates, was polite, and didn't talk in ways that were crude or rude. When I talked to him about God, he seemed interested. *Interested.* Despite all the positive attention I received from him, I couldn't quite figure him out. He said he was a Christian (although his reputation wasn't that of a guy who lived his life for God). His openness to our discussions about God gave me hope that he was what I was looking for. But that day at the gym, I saw him when he was angry, and it was ugly.

As in all the other areas of SPERM, don't evaluate a guy based on isolated moments, but on the totality of those moments combined. Focus on his normal behaviors and attitudes, not on solitary moments of brilliance. Make sure the guy you are interested in is *consistently* godly and kind, in addition to having a good reputation with others, especially his exes. Is he an honest guy, or does he often fudge the truth? Does he drink; does he drink too much? If you are consistently wondering about a guy's character or whether he is telling you the truth, more than likely you have seen something in his behavior that has caused you to doubt him. This is a red flag that should not be ignored. Don't ignore what others say about him and don't try to change him. Granted, if you are interested in a guy and people tell you that he was a troublemaker when he was ten years old, cut the guy some slack. But if his bad reputation comes from recent relationships (like within the past couple of years), remember that any sort of significant change takes time and practice. So if last week he dated your friend and was a jerk to her, don't think that he will act differently with you. He hasn't had enough time to change for the better.

You can find out a lot about a man's character by observing his relationships. Does he have what it takes to commit to one person, or is he a flirt who loves attention? How does he act with his friends? Does he encourage them or put them down in an attempt to make himself look better? Does he have any friends whom you admire—anyone who is a positive influence? The Bible says, "Bad company corrupts good morals," meaning that even if he wants to do good, but consistently surrounds himself with people who have a negative influence on him, he is either already like them or on his way to becoming like them.[1] How does he treat his teachers, coaches, parents, siblings? What kind of social skills does he have? Is he polite? Does he look at your eyes—instead of your body—when he speaks to you? Is he able to express his thoughts and feelings, and does he have the sensitivity and maturity to listen to yours? What are his views of women, other ethnic groups, poor people, pastors, and authority figures? Is he egocentric, ethnocentric, or compassionate toward people who are not like him? How does he talk about his exes or people he doesn't like? Is he arrogant and proud, or is he willing to admit that he doesn't know everything? Does he seek advice from others who are wiser than him, or does he try to figure out everything on his own because he thinks that's what a man is supposed to do? Does he seek knowledge so he can always be right, or is he seeking wisdom and holiness?

Observe how he takes care of himself. Notice his sleeping, eating, exercising, and extracurricular activities. Does he shower, look presentable, and eat healthy? Can he cook and do his own laundry? Does he have a hard time organizing his life and priorities? If he can't take care of himself and make sure his body has what it needs to be healthy, he definitely won't be able to do this for you or your future family.

Lastly, does he have what it takes to be relationally responsible? Your heart deserves to be protected. You deserve attention, priority, and commitment. If he is not responsible and mature in other areas of his life, he won't show the character and integrity that is needed for a man to be responsible for a woman's heart, mind, and body. Bottom line, the way he treats others is the way he will eventually treat you, in due time. Over time people get tired of pretending to be something they are not and their true identity reveals itself. If a guy has a reputation of using women, mooching, being lazy, rude, crude, or hurtful, save your heart and energy for a more worthy man. It is only our pride that lets us think that we are different from his exes, and makes us believe that we will be the one who causes him to change. Pay attention to how he is in his other relationships and relinquish your desire to change him—it is God's job, not yours.

SPERM: Monetary

Money. Singles may not understand how money affects a relationship, but it is one of the main reasons couples argue and file for divorce.[2] Christians know that a fine line separates making the most of what we are given, and pursuing wealth for the allure of power, security, and happiness. When evaluating a guy, the last question to answer is, what are his financial goals and desires? Does he desire wealth, or does he desire to be a good manager of the gifts and talents God gives him? Does he compare his wealth and financial situation to others? Is he always buying the latest electronics, clothes, and cars, or is he okay without all the bling? Do material possessions define his view of himself, or is he happy even if he's driving a twenty-year-old junker? Does he calculate the difference between what he needs and what he wants? Does he have realistic financial expectations? Does he understand the financial responsibilities of a married man? Does he tithe and give to those in need, or is he greedy with his money? Is he generous regardless of the size of his paycheck? Does he have a lot of debt? If so, is he concerned about paying it off and plan to pay it all off?

Some of these questions are hard to answer if the guy is still in school. You may have to infer whether he is or will be responsible with money. If he plays sports, does he complain about not having the newest equipment, shoes, etc., or does he play with what he's given? Does he have any future goals? If so, how is he using the money he earns now to help him achieve those goals? Is he only nice to his parents when he wants money? Does he seem grateful for what he has, or does he stress about getting more things? When he makes money, does he save any of it? Does he spend every paycheck or rack up credit card debt with money he doesn't have?

My mom has been in the banking industry my entire life, so I grew up with an understanding of money. My stepdad, Mark, taught me about working hard for things that were important to me. In high school I started playing golf, and my first set of golf clubs cost a whopping thirty dollars at a local garage sale. After seeing others play, I knew that I wanted, no, I was convinced that I *needed,* expensive clubs like the other girls had. After all, how was I supposed to compete with old-school clubs that didn't have the latest customized weight-distributed face and featherweight shafts? Mark told me that if I couldn't play well with bad clubs, then I wouldn't be able to play that much better with good ones. If I wanted to be good, I would have to practice. We made a deal: if I could shoot a score lower than one hundred, he would buy me brand-new clubs. After I agreed to the deal, Mark said, "Ninety percent of golfers never break a hundred." *Thanks Mark!*

Let's just say that my game needed a *lot* of work, so I put in a *lot* of work. I played in tournaments with girls who had expensive clubs, and to *everyone's* surprise, I played better than they did. Those girls had their "dream clubs" that they used once or twice a week. I had my garage-sale clubs that I used twelve hours a day. I learned that it's not the clubs that make the golfer, just like it isn't the money that makes the man. Instead, it is the integrity and perspective that make it all work. Through the process of becoming a better golfer, I realized the benefit in delaying self-gratification. I worked so hard to get new, state-of-the-art clubs that once I earned them, I never took them for granted.

On a daily basis, practice making yourself wait and work for things instead of just getting it when you want it. By practicing self-discipline in the small things, every area of your life will benefit from it. I think you will either decide you don't really want those things at all, or you will appreciate them so much more when you receive them. Your potential dater should have the willpower to learn the same skills. When you become skilled at practicing the art of delayed gratification, it will dramatically help you avoid sexual temptation.

He's Got SPERM—Now What?

The next time a guy asks you out or simply catches your eye from across a room, remember the acronym SPERM and save yourself from any lingering klutzy tendencies of falling in love. Watch what the guy does, says, and feels. Make sure his words and actions communicate his passion for God. His behavior will either show you that he is seeking God and putting Him first, or not. Before you jump into a dating relationship, be wise in evaluating yourself and that hunk of a man using the five SPERM areas: spiritual, physical, emotional, relational, and monetary. When the wrong guy comes along, you'll be able to evaluate the kind of man he is and walk away when you realize he doesn't measure up. Being honest with yourself while evaluating where a guy fits on the SPERM spectrum can be tricky, so I highly recommend that you find another girl who is passionate about pursuing God and ask her to be your accountability partner. To benefit from the wisdom of those older than you, I also suggest finding a mentor and talking to your parents about a potential dater.

Now that you have the tools to evaluate a man before dating him, we will discuss the fun and tough issues of dating. Oh the drama, drama, drama. Speaking from experience, it can be hell on earth trying to make things work with the wrong guy. SPERM will set you on the right track, but using the SPERM guidelines doesn't guarantee that you won't ever have your heart broken.

CHAPTER 8

My Two Cents About Dating

FOR SOME REASON DATING is very confusing for Christians, so let me clarify the subject by oversimplifying it. We were created by God because He desired to have a loving relationship with us. God gave us a few commands like, "love and obey God," and "love others," but for some reason we don't think these commands apply to our dating lives.[1] Essentially Christian dating should be comprised of two selfless people who encourage each other in their relationship with God. Christian dating should be all about two God-fearing people who are seeking to maintain their purity while slowly getting to know each other with the purpose of seeing if this could be a person God would want them to marry. Christian dating should not be frivolous, misleading, or leave a trail of calloused hearts. Men and women in dating relationships should treat each other with respect, kindness, holiness, and love. All of that said, I have five tips about dating. Let me explain.

Dating Tip #1—Dating Should Be Holy

When dating is godly, it is contagious. People around you will be able to tell that you are seeking to do what God wants you to do simply because you will be growing and maturing in your faith. Maturing in your faith isn't something that happens by taking a class; it is something that is acquired from time spent seeking God and obeying God. When we date the wrong type of guys, we tend to replace what is good and godly for what is vain and worldly. We stop serving God and spend less time reading the Bible and praying, while spending more time trying to convince the wrong guy that we are worthy of being loved.

I have messed up a lot in dating the wrong kind of guys. Sometimes I feel stupid looking back at the guys I dated and wonder, *Why did I date them? Why did it take me so long to see who they really were?* But I don't think I am the only girl who has regrets from past relationships.

I dated a guy who was completely wrong for me for almost three years, but I couldn't see it at first. He spent the majority of the relationship trying to convince me that he was what I was looking for. Instead of paying attention to my doubts, I spent the majority of that relationship giving him the benefit of the doubt. Looking back, I had plenty of reasons to question his sincerity and whether we should continue dating. Instead, I just tried harder to make a bad relationship work. I tried convincing myself that it was enough that he was a "good guy." But that's not enough! I don't want just a "good guy" and I don't want another "nice guy." I want a godly man whose life motivates me to strengthen my relationship with the Lord. In that relationship, I practically had to *beg* my boyfriend to talk to me about what God was doing in his life. I told him I wanted to be in a Bible study together, but he always said he was too busy. After waiting over a year for his life to be "less busy" to have time for a Bible study, I joined a Bible study by myself. It is amazing how dense we can be as women. We stick with a guy longer than we should because we try to be understanding, patient, and loving, when really, the most understanding, patient, and loving thing for both of us is to move on.

If in dating you spend more time wondering about the guy's relationship with God than you do talking to each other about God, it's a good sign that he isn't as serious as you are about his relationship with God. If you are in a dating relationship and find it burdensome to spend time with God, something is likely wrong with your relationship. If God is the most important thing in each of your lives, that shouldn't change just because you are dating. Holy relationships require both individuals' participation. I know it's hard to balance a boyfriend and a busy schedule, but make sure you still spend quality time with God; your dating relationship depends on it. When a man loves God, is reading his Bible frequently, and has friends who are equally as passionate about God, he can't help but talk about God and act in a holy way. Ladies, stop justifying guys' actions and wait for someone who desires to have a holy dating relationship.

SPIRITUAL LEADERSHIP IN HOLY RELATIONSHIPS

When you date a guy committed to loving and obeying Christ and helping you do the same (even in the smallest areas), that type of man will be an excellent spiritual leader. The term "spiritual leader" can be a fuzzy concept to grasp, especially in romantic relationships. Simply put, a good spiritual leader is a man who seeks God and is committed to doing His work. When a man is committed to standing up for the truth, even when no one wants to listen, he is behaving like a spiritual leader. A spiritual leader is committed to prayer and purity. He is the kind of man who prays for you and others constantly. A spiritual leader is someone you can wholeheartedly trust to love, honor, protect, and pray for you. And the funny thing is that a true leader spends the majority of his time not teaching, lecturing, or micromanaging your every move, but simply leading by example.

When my mom and stepdad, Mark, got married it was an adjustment for everyone, to say the least. We remodeled my stepdad's house and three boisterous women moved in, with our dog, Melanie. Mark was outnumbered and he knew it. Sometimes I wonder how he kept from going crazy. But one really cool thing that I observed about Mark was that every day, without missing a beat, he woke up around five o'clock, poured a cup of coffee, picked up his newspaper, Bible, and journal. He read, studied, journaled, and memorized Scripture for what seemed like forever. Of course it only took him ten minutes to get ready for work, so by the time all the ladies in the house were ready to leave, so was he. It was by his example that I started making a habit of reading my Bible more frequently in high school.

A leader is someone who has at least one other person mirroring some aspect of their life. All men are leaders, but the question is, where are they leading us? With the men you choose to date, date the ones who are excited, *no*, passionate about loving God and helping you do the same. Because above all dating should be holy.

HOLY RELATIONSHIPS ARE SEXUALLY PURE

A huge part of dating in a way that is holy and pleasing to God is by keeping our bodies sexually pure. Two verses speak very clearly about being sexually pure: Romans 12:1 says, "Therefore, I urge you, brothers, in view of God's mercy, to offer your bodies as living sacrifices, holy and pleasing to God—this is your spiritual act of worship." And 1 Corinthians 6:18 says to "Flee from sexual immorality. All other sins a man commits are outside his body, but he who sins sexually sins against his own body."

Everyone has a differing opinion about what the sexual boundaries should be in a dating relationship. My thoughts are this: if you are doing something that sexually arouses you or makes you focus on getting sexually aroused, you have crossed the line. If you are flirting with sexual temptation instead of fleeing from it, how is your behavior pleasing God? If you and your boyfriend can't keep from indulging in impure acts or thoughts, then your boundaries aren't high enough. You've crossed the line if after spending time with your boyfriend you go home and feel dirty or wrong about your thoughts or actions. Don't try to "get over" that bad feeling by justifying or ignoring it. Instead change your behavior so that when you go to sleep at night, you do so knowing you have been sexually pure and that God is pleased with your sexual choices. It is so easy to get wrapped up in attraction and lust that we forget about everything else. We forget that God is watching us. And if pleasing God is the main reason we exist and date a guy, then our thoughts, words, and actions must show God that we are in the relationship for Him, not to fulfill our lustful desires.

For the Love of Boundaries

Solomon advised his friends both before and after he married his wife to "not arouse or awaken love until it pleases."[2] The Hebrew word *love* in the above verse means, but is not limited to, sexual affection. Based on the repeated commands throughout the Bible concerning sexual purity, we know that the type of sexual affection that "pleases" God is the kind that happens between a husband and his wife. This verse urges us to protect our heart, mind, *and* body from giving and receiving sexual affection outside of a marriage relationship.

Being sexually pure in our dating relationships is more than just abstaining from sex. Sexual activity impacts more than just our bodies, which is why we need to go one step further in abstaining from *anything* that would "arouse or awaken" our sexual desire before marriage. To avoid premarital sex, we need to avoid the things that lead to sex, both mentally and physically.

A few years ago, my friend Carly asked me for help with set-ting sexual boundaries for her and her fiancé. The boundaries that worked for them while they were dating were not high enough once they were engaged. They were so sexually frustrated that they finally decided they couldn't kiss anymore, he couldn't wear cologne around her, and they couldn't be alone together. From that point on, they always had friends or family around when they spent time together. This is what I call not stirring up or awaking love until it pleases. My friends' sexual boundaries were like those of Solomon and his woman. They were honest with each other about their temptations, and they took the necessary steps to remain sexu-ally pure until they married.

His Sexual Desires

A guy worth dating will do whatever it takes to have other godly men keep him accountable for his emotions and sexual crav-ings. What does he do when he is turned on? How does he handle it? Does he view porn and indulge his masturbation cravings, or does he flee from his emotional temptations and put up protective barriers—Web site accountability programs or regular meetings with a mentor, for example—to keep him from being tempted? Every man struggles with lust, but I encourage you to only date men who are committed to resisting these temptations. Why? Because if he doesn't control himself now, his habits will only get worse. The Bible says it plainly: "But each one is tempted when he is carried away and enticed by his own lust. Then when lust has conceived, it gives birth to sin; and when sin is accomplished, it brings forth death."[3]

When a man views pornographic material, his mind and entire body are corrupted. This pollution, this garbage that is embedded in his memory, will eventually become evident in his words and actions. He will make you feel more like an object than a treasure.

Let me assure you that even if he tells you he is not acting on his lusts now, he will eventually. What a man thinks about will affect his actions, behavior, habits, and lifestyle. So choose a man who is dedicated to keeping his eyes, heart, mind, body, and soul pure. Without a close, personal relationship with God, a man will continue to fill his mind with lustful thoughts that result in his inability to fully appreciate you for who you are: a woman, a daughter of God—not a sex object. When a man controls his thoughts and emotions, you will want to give yourself fully to him in marriage, but not before.

My Boundaries

I have set up certain physical boundaries to keep my mind, body, and soul pure. Currently my sexual boundary is kissing on the lips. But the older I get, the more I wonder if I should even do that. I am not a prude; I am just so easily aroused. I mean c'mon, I get horny just thinking about guys sometimes. Anyway, here are some details associated with the "just kissing" boundary that help me stay pure.

No sex in the city and no . . .

- Kissing for more than thirty seconds, kissing with bodies pressed together, kissing on the ears or anywhere that is not the face, kissing lying down, making sensual noises while kissing, kissing with the intention of arousing me or my man.
- Roaming hands: Hands are allowed on the face, shoulders, and back, but all other places are off limits.
- Spending prolonged time alone with my boyfriend just lying around at one of our houses.
- Spending any time in a bedroom with my boyfriend. The bedroom is off limits. (If you are anything like me, it doesn't matter what you're doing in a bedroom—you could be folding laundry or doing homework—just being in the bedroom makes you think about sex. The whole focus of the room is the bed and eventually getting on it.)

Additional Tips to Stay Pure

Being a thirty-year-old virgin isn't just an accident; I have been purposefully pursuing purity since I can remember. Here are some additional tips that have helped me in my purity pursuit.

Know what the Bible says about sex. Establish your relationship and sexual boundaries based on biblical principles (italics mine):

> For out of the heart come evil thoughts, murder, adultery, *sexual immorality*, theft, false testimony, slander. (Matthew 15:19)

> Instead we should write to them, telling them to abstain from food polluted by idols, from *sexual immorality*, from the meat of strangled animals and from blood. (Acts 15:20)

> Therefore God gave them over in the sinful desires of their hearts to *sexual impurity* for the degrading of their bodies with one another. (Romans 1:24)

> Let us behave decently, as in the daytime, not in orgies and drunkenness, not in *sexual immorality* and debauchery, not in dissension and jealousy. (Romans 13:13)

> I am afraid that when I come again my God will humble me before you, and I will be grieved over many who have sinned earlier and have not repented of the *impurity, sexual* sin and debauchery in which they have indulged. (2 Corinthians 12:21)

> The acts of the sinful nature are obvious: *sexual immorality, impurity* and debauchery. (Galatians 5:19)

> But among you there must not be even a hint of *sexual immorality*, or of any kind of *impurity*, or of greed, because these are improper for God's holy people. (Ephesians 5:3)

> Put to death, therefore, whatever belongs to your earthly nature: *sexual immorality, impurity, lust,* evil desires and greed, which is idolatry. (Colossians 3:5)

Get your parents involved. Let your parents meet guys *before* you agree to go out with them. Your parents will be able to see good and bad qualities in guys that you may not be able to see right away. Their good advice will save you so much heartache and help you stay pure. Let your dad clean his shotgun while grilling the guy a little . . . it is good for both you and your potential suitor.

Find a mentor. My mentors are usually married women who have lived through the dating scene and understand what makes a good marriage. Make sure you're comfortable talking to your mentor about sex. Ask your mentor to help you come up with physical boundaries and practice situations where you need to say no.

Have an accountability partner. You need someone you trust to help hold you to a higher standard; someone who can help you in your walk to stay sexually pure. Find someone you can trust with your secrets; a person who will pray for you and encourage you when you need it.

Discuss your boundaries with your guy. As we've discussed, if he doesn't share your boundaries, thank him for dinner and say, "Sayonara, adios" or "Thanks, but no thanks." Don't wait until he's trying to undo your pants to tell him that you only want to kiss. It will be hard for you to slow the surge of sexual feelings and you'll be vulnerable to him trying to convince you to forget your boundaries.

Give yourself a curfew on your dates. Around 10:00 PM is when the "Horny Monster" usually comes out. When you are tired, you want to lie down and get comfortable. This position is not helpful when you are trying to stay sexually pure. Tell your man he has to leave—you can talk in the morning. When we date guys we *always* lose track of time. I used to have a hard time with this one. After nine o'clock I get tired and want to cuddle. This leads to the temptation to have sex. I finally realized what my problem was and put a stop to it. I started setting my stove timer to go off twenty minutes before my date or boyfriend had to leave. (You know how it can take forever to say goodbye, especially when you are all goo-goo over some guy.) The alarm was a way to remind both of us that it was time to bring closure to our fun night.

Have a chaperone accompany you on dates. Having a friend with you on a date not only helps with safety but also with purity.

Pillows are your best friend. If you want to cuddle with your boyfriend, do it while in the seated position and with lots of pillows in between you to act as a barrier. Seriously, they help! You can snuggle without crossing any lines mentally or sexually. It's hard to think about sex if you can't feel anything but his arms around you. If pillows don't work, use blankets. I know it sounds weird, but it works. If you are having a tough time keeping your hands to yourself, swaddle yourself (or him) in a blanket like you do a newborn baby, and then sit next to the guy. It's impossible for you to do something with your arms or legs when they are all tucked in . . . and it looks hilarious!

Keep your mind pure. Even when I am alone, sexual thoughts come to mind. When this happens, I stop it immediately and think of something else. I am not sure why, but sometimes this is harder than other times; so when I am really feeling tempted, I turn on Christian music and pray for God to purify my thoughts. Sometimes if it is *really* bad, I call a friend and talk to them about my issue.

Dress appropriately. Communicate your purity stance and dating boundaries with your clothes! It is easier to convince guys that you are serious about staying sexually pure when you have appropriate clothes on. Don't wear shirts that look like bikini tops or skirts that look like belts. Cover your body and save a little for the imagination. Contrary to popular opinion, just because you have a hot body does *not* mean you need to flaunt it.

Have an open-door policy. If you and your boyfriend are in a room alone, keep the door open. You can still get to know each other with the door open, but this way you are controlling your urges for an all-out make-out session. Also, the open-door policy leaves no room for anyone to wonder what you are doing—that's being above reproach, avoiding the appearance of wrongdoing.

Discuss your physical boundaries with a guy, but don't discuss sexual topics. Don't daily talk about the sexual acts you are dying to do with each other. You'll have a time and a place to do this in premarital counseling. While dating, if every day the guy tells you how badly he wants to have sex with you, either he needs to stop communicating his sexual desires with you, or he views you as a sex object and you need to end the relationship. I know what it's like to be horny (hello, have you read this book?), but sex is not the topic of my discussions with my boyfriends. There are too many other amazing, God-honoring things to talk about.

Discuss your sexual pasts. Let me explain. As you get closer to marriage it is important to have a "tell all" discussion about your sexual pasts—not the kiss-by-kiss details, but a general description of your sexual histories. This conversation may hurt you and him, but the honesty and forgiveness that results will bring you closer. After having this talk, let it rest. Forgive each other and don't bring it up again. Don't use this information against him in the future unless you realize he hasn't changed and is acting in the same negative pattern toward you.

Don't play house. Don't spend the night or sleep over, and don't move in together. Not only is cohabiting against biblical principles, but there are numerous statistics that show it doesn't help two people have a successful marriage.[4]

Move slow. You have the rest of your married life to make out; don't feel like you need to be doing that stuff now.

Remember, people are watching you! What you do, they will do. The Bible warns us against doing something that could cause anyone to stumble (and we definitely don't want to do something that isn't pleasing to God).[5]

Dating Tip #2—Dating Should Be Safe

Depending on your age and how long you have known a guy before he asks you out will dramatically affect this dating ideal. You never know how God may bring you your future husband, but for all the men you date, safety should be a priority.

Although dating and meeting new people can be fun and exciting, we have to remember that there are a lot of weirdos out there. I can't stress how important it is to date safely. Be careful about what information you put on your Web sites, blogs, texts, etc. It is always the guy you *don't* want calling you who will . . . over and over and over again. In college a couple of girls on my floor met guys on a bus, at a party, wherever, and gave them their phone number. The guys found out their address and started stalking them. The police had to get involved and the girls lived in fear. This stuff really happens, so be wise about who you give personal information to.

One of my roommates was asked out by her fellow snowboard instructor one day while she was working. He said he wanted to go boarding with her about three hours away. He would pick her up at our house and drop her off. She agreed and thought nothing of it. Sounds fun, right? When I spoke with my roommate about her potential date and warned her about the situation, she got mad at me and said, "I am a grown woman," to which I responded, "Grown women get kidnapped and date-raped everyday." You see, if something were to happen to her, I would have nothing to tell the police. She didn't know the guy's last name, what car he drove, how old he was, where he lived, or anything about his background. Yet she was willing to drive in a car with him for three hours each way in a snowstorm. After we talked about it a little more, she decided not to go out with him. Because women tend to be trusting, we forget that some people act maliciously toward women, which is why we should be cautious about who we go out with and where we go with them. We should dig a little deeper before we agree to certain situations.

One of my friends in college liked to go to dance clubs with her group of girlfriends. Twice while she was in the club someone slipped a roofie (aka the date-rape drug) into her drink. Both times it made her feel very drunk; the next morning she couldn't remember *anything* that happened the night before. Another girl I knew from high school went to a party with a couple of popular guys she knew from her school, and they both ended up raping her that night. She never filed any charges because she was afraid of being unpopular. We need to make wise dating decisions because most of us aren't as physically strong as the guys who ask us out on dates (think about it, most of us weigh nothing in comparison). Part of making wise decisions is demanding respect and insisting on being treated like a lady. When we do this, men usually respond accordingly.

Once you live outside of your parents' home, you have to come up with creative ways to safely date. Another one of my roommates in college was asked out while working as a coffee barista. The guy was nice and super cute, so she agreed. When she came home to tell us the good news—getting asked out is always good news—all four roommates came up with a safe date spot. Instead of having him pick her up at her house, which is what a gentleman should offer to do, she suggested meeting him at a public place and told him that she was bringing a few of her friends. He agreed to do the same. There were a total of ten of us sitting together to celebrate my friend's hot date. It was hilarious. He brought three of his buddies and the rest were our friends. All of the roomies talked with his friends while my roommate enjoyed conversation with her date.

Inviting my friends to be my chaperones on dates has been fun and helpful. They don't go everywhere with me, but they are always on call. Lately the key component to fun dates has been my friends, so I decided that they should be rewarded. When I get asked out I tell my date to bring a handsome Christian man for my friend as well. Why not? So far my girlfriends have accompanied me surfing, salsa dancing, and sailing. What a blast! Now we take turns being the chaperone—and we love it.

Some people may think some or all of these safe dating practices are extreme, but I find it much easier to be safe than to learn the hard way. Besides, it's more fun to be creative on dates rather than just going to dinner and a movie or coffee with a complete stranger.

Dating Tip #3—Dating Should Be Adventurous

In the summer of 2008, I started working in the furniture department of Crate & Barrel in San Diego, California. Because not one of my guy friends had ever heard of this company, I expected the majority of my customers to be women. Much to my surprise, selling furniture is a great way to meet single, straight, good-looking men. *Who knew?* My first day on the sales floor, I noticed a guy looking at a sofa and thought he needed help. So I asked him if he had any questions. He didn't and I moved on. At first I didn't even notice that he was my age, incredibly good-looking, and totally ripped. Later he tracked me down to ask a few questions. Initially, his questions were focused on the sofa, but they quickly went to questions about me. I talked about how much I love to surf and love being in the water. He talked with me a long time about everything *but* the sofa he wanted.

I wear my purity ring on my right hand with a fish ring right next to it. While I was ringing up his order he asked me about the fish ring, and I decided to tell him about my purity ring as well . . . mostly because it's fun to see guys' reactions when they hear that I'm not having sex until I am married. But I also wanted to see if my purity stance would scare him away. I handed him his paperwork and thanked him for coming to the store. As he started walking away, he looked like he had more questions. Thinking he needed to know more about the delivery process, I asked him, "Do you have other questions?" and he responded with, "Yeah, I want to know if you will go surfing with me sometime." I thought I scared him away with all my talk about being a Christian and a virgin, but nope, he still asked me out.

When I agreed to go surfing with him he said, "Great, can I have your number?" Well, I don't give my number to guys I don't know. There are a lot of weirdos out there. So this is how our conversation went:

"Can I get your phone number?"

"I don't give out my number to guys I don't know."

"So can I give you mine?"

"No, I am really old-fashioned and I don't think it's my job to call a guy."

"Hmm, so how can I get ahold of you?"

"You can have my e-mail address and we can go from there."

He agreed and said, "So what, I get your number on the third date?"

I looked at him with a smile on my face and said, "Only if you're lucky."

He smiled at me and I thought, *I won't hear from him, but it was fun getting asked out.* Needless to say, I was shocked when he e-mailed me a couple days later. My friend Kristen and I went surfing with him, and we had a blast. That date was an adventure. I met someone new, hiked down cliffs with my board, backpack, and snacks in hand, surfed for the first time in a long time, and got to hang with my best friend, Kristen. It doesn't get any better than that!

I know a lot of guys choose coffee shops for the first date. I agree that this is a nice, safe way to try to meet a girl and have a meaningful conversation with her. But for us ladies who don't drink coffee, it's a tough first date. I went on a coffee date once and I almost fell asleep because the hot cocoa was, well, hot, the lights were low, and the relaxing music was a little too soothing. After a few minutes in that environment I was ready to cuddle up with a blanket on my sofa. (Maybe I should have ordered some coffee after all.) Recently I was asked out for coffee and I told the guy I would rather do something active. We ended up meeting at a photo gallery, setting our friends up on a blind date, and having a great time talking over dinner.

Don't get me wrong, I love a good chai tea latte and a Rice Krispies treat, but where's the spontaneity in that? I live in San Diego—there are so many inexpensive, fun things to do. Instead of sitting in a coffee shop, I want to learn indoor rock climbing, rent a paddleboat or kayaks, or enjoy a free concert.

Dating should be fun. So what if you get set up on a blind date with a "dork" who insists on taking you to his favorite hamburger place, Fuddruckers? If anything, you get a good story out of it and the chance to work on your interpersonal communication skills. It's good to go to new places and meet new people. Life is supposed to be an adventure, so why should dating be any different?

Dating Tip #4—Dating Should Be Purposeful

Dating five guys at the same time with the sole purpose of finding the best kisser is *not* the kind of dating I am promoting. As I mentioned earlier, we need to treat each other with love and kindness. The person you date, even if you only go out once, should be a better person because of the experience. Remember that every man you date (but one) will be your ex, so treat men in a way that *their* future spouse will appreciate. Christian dating relationships should be distinctly different from those relationships we see in Hollywood. I believe as Christians we should date with a purpose. This purpose is to find someone who we are excited to marry and commit the rest of our life to.

THE DTR TALK

Whether we realize what we are doing or not, we are quick to evaluate and label guys (e.g., hot, dorky, annoying, funny). During the date, we'll be trying to put the guy into one of four categories. These four categories (from the worst to best) are:

> #4 Please lose my number.

> #3 Nice guy—not my type but I want to set him up with my friend.

> #2 I would go out with him again; we had a good connection.

> #1 Our kids would be gorgeous and his last name sounds good with my first name!

Initially we draw conclusions about his mannerisms and personality, but figuring out if he is husband material takes time. The first date is really a test to see if he will make it to a second date.

After several dates and in-depth discussions, I think it's important to have a DTR. DTR stands for the Defining the Relationship talk. In order to date purposefully, you have to honestly communicate with each other about your thoughts and feelings about the relationship.

If you know that you are not interested in a guy romantically, it is best to tell him as soon as possible. With gentleness and sensitivity affirm his positive attributes, but don't lead him on or let him take you on more dates. Tell him the truth. (One of my stepdad's favorite Bible verses is John 8:32, "The truth will set you free," the perfect dating principle.) Don't just stop calling a guy back. My friends and I have been on the receiving end of relationships where we wondered why a guy didn't call more, was suddenly rude, or led us on only to see him out with another girl later that week. We don't want to *discover* that he doesn't like us, and we don't want to feel used after going out of our way to do nice things for him. We would rather know the truth even when the truth hurts. So don't be rude in hopes that he figures out you don't like him. Instead be respectful, speak the truth in love, and have the DTR. Both of you will be glad that you did, even if he is too immature to realize it at the time.

Although I have gotten better at having DTRs, they can be hard. I don't like hurting a guy's feelings and I don't like having my feelings hurt either. But the cool thing about DTRs is that *sometimes* they can go really well.

THE INTERVIEW

Sometimes the godly guy you like, likes you back. (I know, I know, this sounds surreal to most of us.) The phenomena of liking someone who likes you *and* is good for you is not something that many of us single ladies have experienced, but it can totally happen. In the past when I have had this type of conversation with a man, and it turned out that we both really liked each other, we began talking about the next steps. Since we should date with a purpose, the purpose of our DTR is to see if we should be just friends or take our relationship to the next level. For me this next level is becoming boyfriend and girlfriend. In some Christian circles they title this stage "courtship." It is a big deal for me to be someone's girlfriend, so before I agree to take the dating relationship to the next level, there are a few people my guy needs to meet first. Unlike in the movies, I think guys should meet the family long before there is ever talk of getting engaged.

In the past, before a guy could become my boyfriend, he first had to meet my stepdad, Mark. It wasn't anything big, just a little man-to-man chat that ended with Mark cleaning his shotgun as he made sure no one hurt his baby girl. Okay, so Mark didn't threaten anyone, but it sure made me feel special knowing that he loved me enough to get to know the guy who wanted to date me. But since my stepdad died in 2005 from lung cancer, I have recruited people to interview my dates. Every girl needs a fatherly figure to interrogate her dates and help her weed out the bad ones. When I lived in Colorado, Pastor Gene was good at this sort of thing. I've also had friends interview my dates. They went out for coffee and asked him important questions. After every interview both my friends and pastors told me what they thought about the guy. Their words usually confirmed my preexisting concerns and impressions. Besides those conducting the interviews, I like my guy to meet my mom, sister, accountability partner, and mentor.

Only once did I continue to date a guy who didn't pass an interview with flying colors. We dated long distance, and it was several months before my pastor had a one-on-one with him. His immaturity was apparent to my pastor. Had I known how his immaturity would negatively impact me, I would have ended the relationship after he met with my pastor. Even though that relationship was like hell on earth, through it God taught me a lot about myself and how I deserve to be treated by men.

There have been guys along the way who didn't like having to meet with these people to discuss me and our relationship, and it was always these guys who didn't pass the test. There are reasons why guys don't want to meet your family, and for me it has always been because they knew they were not the type of man that I deserved.

A FIGHT FOR LOVE

As a relationship progresses and you reveal more about yourself to your man, disagreements will occur, and when they do, love and patience are needed in order for the relationship to work. In a romantic relationship, a woman's heart is won over when she is with a man she trusts; a man who desires to be like Jesus in every area of his life. This kind of man is one who is kind and loving even when he is upset. If you can't disagree about something without him insulting and embarrassing you, then he is not the right guy for you. You should be able to discuss your differences in a mature way. Even when you are arguing, you ought to be communicating that you love and care for each other. Find a man who will validate your feelings and try to understand you better. Don't get me wrong, I am not giving you permission to act like a crazy woman when things don't go your way; I am only saying it is okay to have feelings. You know you have found a good guy when you feel safe to express your emotions around him. When you feel free to laugh, cry, or be sad or silly around a guy, you have found a guy who is probably in touch with his emotions and capable of loving you even when your emotions confuse him.

LOVE, REAL LOVE

We want to date and marry a man because we want to love and be loved, but do we really know what love is? How do you know if you are really in love? The Bible talks about love—a lot. I can never read these verses enough.

> Love is patient, love is kind and is not jealous; love does
> not brag and is not arrogant, does not act unbecomingly;
> it does not seek its own, is not provoked, does not
> take into account a wrong suffered, does not rejoice in
> unrighteousness, but rejoices with the truth; bears all

things, believes all things, hopes all things, endures all
things. Love never fails. (1 Corinthians 13:4–8a)

In these verses we are reminded that love takes effort, dedication,
time, thought, and planning. Love will require a daily vow of waking
up and reminding yourself, "Today I will do my best to love my
husband in all sixteen ways that the Bible mentions." Contrary to
the "happily ever after" motto you see in the Cinderella movies, you
won't always wake up *feeling* in love with your spouse. Some days
you won't want to live in the same house as him. Why do you think
the Bible commands a husband to love his wife, and instructs a wife
to respect her husband?[6] Some days you will not *feel* like respecting
your husband, and he will not *feel* like living in the same house as
you. But when love is based on more than fleeting feelings, emotions,
or physical attraction, it has the opportunity to last "as long as you
both shall live." Love should be a bold, selfless, purposeful, daily
choice. To have a loving marriage in the future, we need to practice
loving people now.

Dating Tip #5—Don't Date a Guy's *Potential*

A lot of guys out there have a lot of potential of becoming great, but
that is not enough of a reason to date them. I have had more than a
few guys tell me, "When I get married, *then* I will ——" You fill in
the blank because you have probably heard this too. Guys swear that
when they get married they will be cleaner, on time, more romantic,
better with their finances, more apt to cook and work out, and ready
to spend more time with their woman. Although these goals are
commendable, they sound more like New Year's resolutions than
reasons for ladies to date them. If a guy eats junk food now, he will
most likely continue eating poorly. If he is messy and unorganized
now, he will probably stay the same or get messier.

If a person wants to be better at something, like eating healthy, exercising, planning, and prioritizing, he or she has to work at it. Habits don't form overnight. And last I checked, there aren't any "anti-messy inhalers," "junk-food vaccines," or "punctual pills" you can give the guy you're dating. For someone to be different from who they are today, he or she needs to have a change of heart and practice new habits. For example, if a man wants his home to be clean, he needs a goal, a plan, cleaning supplies, an alarm clock, and the desire to get rid of a few things. He will need to wake up earlier in the morning to have extra time to make the bed and put his stuff away. He should practice being clean while he lives with his parents and roommates. He can't push a magical "just married" button that will automatically change him into the organized, clean, and healthy guy that he wants to be once he's married. Don't fool yourself. No one changes in a day. Change requires goals, a plan, prayer, and daily practice.

This is especially important to remember when we consider the guy we're dating. I get mad when my friends tell me they are dating a guy who is sweet to them *sometimes* and really mean at other times. The good times are so "nice" that they try to forget when he is mean. The worst is when girls say, "But the sex is so good. We are perfect for each other." *What?* They try to forget that he doesn't call when he says he will or that he lies to them. Like the time a boyfriend told me he wanted to try harder on our relationship, and that same night he stood me up to get drunk with his friends. Ladies, for a guy to deserve to spend prolonged time with you, he needs to be consistently nice, trustworthy, respectful, and reliable. Healthy, happy, godly marriages are a direct result of healthy, happy, godly dating relationships; they don't come from dating relationships that feel like roller coasters. If your guy is inconsistent in his words, actions, and his devotion to God or to you when you are dating, don't think he will improve in marriage.

Don't date a guy based on his potential. Date a guy based on who he is today. Who he is and the decisions he makes today will determine who he will be in the future. If he is a liar and a cheat when you are dating, ladies, he will be a liar and a cheat later.

Dating should be holy, safe, adventurous, and purposeful. If after dating a guy for a while, you see red flags or warning signs that he isn't good enough for you, stop thinking about how sweet he was when you first started dating, face the truth about what he's like today, and get out of that relationship. From what you see consistently in your dating relationship, is this guy's "best" good enough for you? If he doesn't make time to love you and serve you in a dating relationship, marriage will feel like prison.

Now that we've discussed dating and love, we have to talk about the three magical words, "I am engaged!" From what I hear, after a man gets down on one knee and confesses his undying love for her, a switch flips in a woman's body, generating a current of excitement about the future. But with the excitement comes fear, the "what ifs" that can flood a girl's mind. What if she isn't a good wife, mom, lover . . . what if? In the next chapter we will explore real-life wedding jitters as well as the excitement that a woman should feel when she is marrying the best man she has ever known.

CHAPTER 9

The One-Eyed Snake
and Other Pre-Honeymoon Fears

A LOT HAPPENS TO A WOMAN when she transitions from being a girlfriend to a fiancée. She begins picking her bridesmaids, choosing a church, sending invitations, ordering cakes, deciding between chicken or beef, buying flowers, and finding the perfect dress. This is all great fun, but she has other thoughts on her mind too, thoughts that most people don't talk about—so of course I will talk about them.

Honeymoon Preparations

Every woman is insecure about something and wonders what her future husband will think about her imperfections. She wonders how bright the lights will be in their honeymoon suite and what expression her new husband will have on his face when he sees her naked for the first time.

So what can we do to prepare during the days and months leading up to the wedding? (I highly recommend couples go through
premarital counseling *before* they get engaged. Once engaged, your
mind should be geared toward the details of the wedding and marriage preparations, not wondering, *Do I really like this guy?*) After
one of my friends got engaged she told me she was on the LGN
diet—Look Good Naked. Other couples I know got memberships
at tanning salons and gyms. The whole tanning bed thing sounded
pretty weird to me until I started to think about it. I spend a lot of
time playing in the ocean and I always have a tan line. I don't want
to be stark white with a funky tan line the first time I get naked
with my husband; for some reason that doesn't seem romantic to
me. All of these ideas sound great for a woman's physical preparations for marriage, but how does a fiancée prepare herself emotionally and mentally for this whole "shameless oneness" thing? I am a
confident person, but I too have insecurities. I love to sing, but I do
not like singing in front of people (I am no Carrie Underwood). I
am thin and pretty, but I wouldn't say I am a supermodel. When I
work out, I sweat. When I wake up in the morning, I have morning breath. I have a period every month and sometimes my face
breaks out. I have insecurities just like everyone else. So how can
we realistically prepare for being naked—with the lights on—with
our future husbands?

My Own Insecurities

This area, like all areas we need to work on, we must first take to God
and ask Him to help us. In some cases He will have to reprogram
our thinking, and our eyes, in how we look at our bodies. In other
cases, we may just need to make some adjustments to our lifestyle
and acquaintances.

In junior high, I felt like my life was out of control, so I did what
many girls do in that stage of life—I decided to control my food.

I had an awful relationship with my dad and junior high was hell at times. Convinced that I was fat, I became obsessed with being thin. I cut out pictures of Victoria's Secret models and put them on the pantry and refrigerator, so when I would get hungry I would be reminded of why I shouldn't eat. Had I known anything about nutrition and how the body reacts when we don't give it the food it needs for energy, I hope I would have acted differently. At that point, I started seeing a counselor to help me with my self-esteem and eating problems. When we get engaged, we suddenly start experiencing those junior high insecurities again.

In high school I realized that when I looked at magazines or watched popular TV shows, I began to feel less attractive. After all, I don't look like those airbrushed girls; in fact, the models themselves don't even look like their pictures. In contrast, I noticed that when I hang around positive and encouraging people, my self-esteem goes up and I feel better about myself. When I date quality guys, the ones who see the beauty that radiates from the inside out, the kind of men who make you feel loved and beautiful whether you are wearing a cocktail dress or a wet suit, I feel prettier than when I go on dates with guys who are overly concerned about their looks.

I modeled for about a day before I realized it was not my thing. I have pictures from photo shoots that were edited to the point that they don't even look like me. Some of my freckles were erased, my boobs were enlarged, and parts of my thighs were cut off to make me look thinner. I don't know why I was shocked when I saw my pictures; stuff like that happens every day. Designers and photo editors do the same thing to every woman they put on magazine covers—they edit so much that the end result is fake. How sad it must be for a model or actress to see her image on the cover of a magazine, cropped and edited so that she doesn't even recognize herself. It's as if the magazine companies are saying, "You just aren't cute enough and you need some tweaking." What if my husband thinks I need some "tweaking"?

I eat healthy, exercise regularly, and am in good shape. But I am modest and shy; I'm not the type to walk on the beach with just my swimsuit on. First, I don't trust swimsuits—they hardly ever stay in the places they are supposed to. Second, I feel better with clothes on. I just don't feel comfortable jumping, sitting, swimming, surfing, or walking around when I am practically naked.

I competed in San Diego's Miss America pageant during my first year living in California. The first portion of the show was our talent; next was the swimsuit portion. Whoop-de-do . . . *not really*. I was supposed to walk to the center of the stage (with the awful overhead lighting), take off this little sash thing that was tied around my waist, and then do a couple loops around the stage, all while wearing high heels. I was mortified. I kept thinking, *Why did I decide to do this?* (I did it because I wanted to get my master's degree and didn't want to pay for it. Depending on how far you get in the competition, you can earn varying amounts of scholarship money.) When I walked out to center stage, I heard shouts and applause and my face turned bright red. *Are they joking? I don't look that good in a swimsuit.* Then I began to think of my guy friends who said they were coming to watch the pageant. I almost ran off the stage. Afterward I was close to hyperventilating and I vowed never to do something like that again. This scenario is what comes to mind when I think of my husband seeing me naked for the first time. How will I feel when he wants to look at every area of my body? Right now I am not ready for all of that. It's weird—I am ready for sex, but not all of the other stuff . . . I think I need to work on this.

So what can I do to "work on it," and what can I do to realistically prepare for my husband and giving myself completely to him? Most likely he will have flaws just like everyone else: bulges, sags, spots, etc. Although I am very curious, I have heard that the penis is not the most *captivating* thing to look at. They don't call it the "one-eyed snake" for nothing. I think men's bodies look great under clothes, but what if I don't like what I see on my wedding night? I talked to some of my married friends—they know I come up with crazy questions—and they were honest with me. They said the insecurities don't just go away when you get married. Again, there is no magic "married" button that fixes everything.

What If He Doesn't Like What He Sees?

It was just another day of school and homework when I was suddenly surprised by my boyfriend standing outside my classroom holding a bouquet of flowers. He was in town for a month to see me, while taking a break from full-time missionary service. The night before, I had mentioned that I was going to buy my books the next day at school, so he surprised me after my last class and insisted on carrying all my books for me. He didn't want me to have to carry them across campus by myself. *Cute, huh?* After going to the bookstore, we walked to my car, hand in hand, heart in heart. I could have floated away on a cloud as the wind lightly blew the hair off my face. It was so romantic, and then he spoke. "Finally your hair is off your forehead. I hate your bangs." *What the heck? Was that supposed to be a compliment?* Another time he told me that he used to tell his cousin (who was really overweight) that she had "good child-bearing hips." That was his way of saying she was big. I guess he and his other cousins used to laugh about it a lot. Well, I think he forgot that he told me this story because one day he told me the same thing. I was so embarrassed. I was a size four, and I felt so ugly and insecure I didn't know what to do. If it were some random stranger who said these things to me, the words probably would not have affected me as much. But when hurtful words like that came from the man who told me he loved me, my natural reaction was to withdraw and to try to protect myself.

Three months after he visited me and returned to the mission field, I realized that I felt ugly. I hadn't struggled with feeling insecure and ugly for years, but suddenly the feelings flooded back. These negative thoughts were so loud in my mind that even when I did feel cute, those thoughts lasted only a few minutes. So, I spent some time with the Lord to figure out why I felt so ugly. When I realized how my boyfriend's negative comments affected me, I was shocked. While he was in town I tried to make the most of the situation, so I didn't express my hurt feelings. I didn't even know I was hurt right away, I think I was still in shock. I definitely didn't realize how much of a negative impact his words had on my self-esteem. He said I shouldn't wear makeup (I *like* to wear makeup). He didn't like my hair color, hair length, or hair cut. He thought I was too thin. A couple months later he thought I was out of shape. A month later, he thought I was getting too muscular and shouldn't work out as much. Sorry, my body doesn't change that much *ever*, let alone in one or two months. But on and on it went for the month that he was in town and the five months after that as we communicated by phone and e-mail. Sometimes when I think about giving my whole heart to a man in marriage I get a little nervous and wonder how I will be able to deal with my insecurities as they arise.

To halt the negative voices in my mind, I did something that my stepdad taught me to do when I was in high school. Every day before I left for school I looked at myself in the mirror and said, "Lindsey, you are beautiful." I wouldn't let myself leave until I believed it. Each day I found something beautiful about myself until I was able to look at myself in the mirror, smile, and really believe that I was beautiful. After we broke up I was so grateful that I didn't marry him! I couldn't have imagined giving myself fully to this kind of a man. I have dated a couple of guys who I thought I wanted to marry, but with both guys I felt uneasy about giving myself completely to them in marriage. I just wasn't convinced that they would love me, all of me. When men don't have realistic expectations of what a real woman's body looks like, they won't be able to appreciate and admire yours. And they definitely won't make you feel beautiful.

They will be the ones who are constantly trying to make you look like a Barbie doll.

I have known men who have made me feel completely accepted, beautiful, and loved. These men have a way of making you feel like you are the most important, most beautiful woman who ever existed. Of course we are not deceived, there is no way we could be the most beautiful woman who ever existed, but we believe it enough to know that we are loved.

Don't freak out about your insecurities, everybody has them. Instead, focus on your qualities that are perfectly unique to you; all the things that make you 100 percent worthy of being fully loved. The engagement period is not the time to settle for less than you deserve. Wait for the right guy so you too can experience the blessing of marriage. I don't have this all figured out but I do know that when it's the right guy, you will feel more at ease in this area.

God's work in our lives is interesting. One thing I have come to understand about God and His timing is this: He will give you the grace to deal with a situation when that situation arises. You don't really need the grace for it beforehand—you just need faith. So by faith, we trust that God's grace will give us the ability to encounter all sorts of unknowns in the future, even the "one-eyed snake." We need to trust God to guide and provide for us. When we submit our entire lives to Him, He will guide us to the right kind of guy for us. He will help us marry a man who is godly, mature, and gracious, who will help us build our self-esteem in our weaker areas. God will show us how He loves us just the way He created us, and our real beauty is defined by what God says about us, not by what magazines say we should be.

Get Ready

You have been so patient, and now the wait is almost over. In the next chapter we get to the really good stuff, the pleasures of two people who waited for sex, are in love, and ready for a good dose of sex! Many people don't know that the Bible talks about good, godly sex because they either haven't read much of the Bible, or they don't understand what they read. Consistently throughout the Bible, God glorifies, edifies, and in some verses He commands married couples to enjoy the pleasures of sex in the marriage relationship (that is so cool!).

In previous chapters we have focused on sex and its consequences when it happens outside of marriage. We have talked about what to look for in a man and tips for dating and purity. Now it's all about experiencing and communicating the sexual pleasures in marriage. I think you will be surprised when I unveil the thoughts, details, and blessings God gave us when He created husband and wife. Find a comfortable sofa and get your hot cocoa, popcorn, and blanket, because you won't want to do anything until you finish reading and rereading chapter 10. It's better than going to the movies.

Sex, Please

Thank You, Jesus!

HAVE YOU EVER READ SOMETHING and thought it sounded sweet and romantic, but had *no* idea what was *really* being said? I felt this way the first time I read the Song of Solomon, an Old Testament book in the Bible. I don't know about you, but any time I read something that uses the words "thou," "thee," or "doest," accompanied by poetic language, I immediately start falling asleep.

One day in college I told my guy friend that I was reading the Song of Solomon and he said, "Oh, the sex book in the Bible." I looked at him funny and we started talking about something else. But he got me thinking . . . I didn't know there was a *sex* book in the Bible. Later that night as soon as I got home, I continued reading that "sex" book. But when I read it, it didn't seem like it was about sex. The two main characters talked back and forth and said things like, "your teeth look like goats' teeth," and "your face looks like fruit," or "your neck looks like a watchtower." *What the heck?* Surely my friend was mistaken, this book is not about sex. Since that day I began researching this weird book, because if there really is a book in the Bible that talked about sex, I wanted to read it . . . without falling asleep.

I found out that the author and main character of this book is King Solomon, a man who in other books of the Bible is described as incredibly handsome and the wisest man to ever live (that is, until Jesus came along, of course). He was strong and yet he chose to deliver his song of love with a delicate balance of romance, intrigue, and sensitivity.

If you aren't familiar with the "sex" book in the Bible, let me be the first to introduce you to this couple and their fabulous story, and show you what they can teach us about sex within the marriage relationship. In the Song of Solomon, all of us girly girls are given multiple reasons to get excited about marrying a loving, strong, and romantic man and having sweet sex with him. Solomon's love interest in the Song of Solomon is the woman he refers to as the Shulamite woman, who eventually becomes his bride. Although this couple was not perfect, they laid an amazing foundation for their marriage by remaining sexually pure until their wedding night. As we have discussed in the previous chapters, great sex in marriage begins with great boundaries before marriage. By keeping his bride sexually pure until their wedding day, Solomon romanced his wife long before they said, "I do." Throughout the entire book, Solomon showed consistency in his character and his words. He communicated his feelings for her and he helped increase her self-esteem.

This couple postponed their sexual longings. They had a traditional Jewish engagement,[1] and now we get front-row seats as we watch what happened on their wedding night—everything from the foreplay to the godly sex. They are about to experience the excitement, pleasure, power, and purpose of sex when it is saved for marriage. If you are anything like me, every couple of pages you will need to calm down and breathe for a second, because this text can get pretty descriptive in some parts. It is clear to me that when Solomon wrote the Song of Solomon, he wanted everyone to know that sex in marriage is supposed to be fun, exciting, and sensual.

Sex and the Sexes

We all know that men are not like women. When most men want sex from their wives, their natural tendencies lead them to say something "romantic" like, "So, uh . . . you wanna have sex or what?" Although men *think* they are being romantic, what a woman really wants to hear is that she is the best thing that's ever happened to him. She wants to hear how he admires her character and beauty. She wants to be romanced; she wants her husband to be creative, sensitive, and loving as he leads them into sexual unity.

Before a husband connects with his wife sexually, she first wants to be connected with his heart. She wants her husband to say, "You are valuable, honorable, and worthy of everything wonderful. Your love for God and others inspires and encourages me to be more like God. Each day I get to know you, my love and admiration for you deepens as I realize how complex and deep you are as a godly woman, my friend, and my wife. I cherish every minute God gives me with you and I pray that He will give us many more minutes like this one." That's what really gets a godly woman turned on. When a wife senses that she is a valuable priority to her husband and she observes how he makes every effort to nourish, notice, and help her, she naturally desires to give him sexual pleasure. Solomon, in all his wisdom, wrote Song of Solomon to explain that sex is good, godly, erotic, and pleasurable for *both* the husband and wife.

The Wedding Day

Solomon went out of his way to *woo* his bride-to-be. He held nothing back as he lavished his fiancée with loving words, adoration, and gifts. This woman wasn't fooled or tricked into liking a guy who wasn't good for her. Solomon was a highly respected man. He waited for his bride until their wedding day, then he went to her, exchanged vows in front of God and everyone, and as everyone else headed straight to their wedding celebration, the newlyweds escaped the crowd to pursue their own party.

The typical Jewish wedding during Solomon's day was on a Tuesday and the celebration lasted at least a week. In our society we say "I do" and rush off to be by ourselves. Today's average bride and groom fly in families and friends from around the country, and then see them for a few brief moments as they stop by their table at the wedding reception. I'd rather celebrate the Jewish way with the tents, bands, feasts, family, and friends for a week. By the time most American couples get to their honeymoon suite on their wedding night, they are tired and exhausted from the day. Unlike our tradition, Solomon and his bride were in no hurry to mingle with friends and family because they knew they would see them throughout the week. Instead of dancing, eating cake, taking pictures, making toasts, and tossing the bouquet, this couple had the freedom to get right to the honeymoon suite, which is where we will pick up in Song of Solomon.

The Honeymoon Suite

Solomon took his bride's hand and escorted her to their private, secluded room, away from the party. They were finally alone and ready to have their *own* feast. Their sexual drought lasted long enough and they were ready to be refreshed. They were ready for sex, but Solomon didn't jump right into sex. Just as Solomon was the leader in the relationship before they married, he continued to lead in his marriage. First we see how Solomon initiated a *conversation* with his new bride. She could have been nervous, scared, anxious, excited, or all of the above. By initiating conversation, he was being tender and sensitive with her. Solomon didn't focus his attention on his needs and demand that his wife perform sexual favors for him. Instead he chose to romance her. He chose to caress her heart before caressing her body.

Solomon used his words to affirm, relax, and arouse his wife. Watch what he does. I can picture him holding his new bride, eyes wide open as he admires her beauty. He probably held her in silence for a little while and then started encouraging her. Solomon began with sincere but vague compliments then moved to more specific details of his adoration. Let's look at the following text from chapter 4 and then I will elaborate on it.

[1]How beautiful you are, my darling,
How beautiful you are!
Your eyes are like doves behind your veil;
Your hair is like a flock of goats
That have descended from Mount Gilead.
[2]Your teeth are like a flock of newly shorn ewes
Which have come up from their washing,
All of which bear twins,
And not one among them has lost her young.
[3]Your lips are like a scarlet thread,
And your mouth is lovely.
Your temples are like a slice of a pomegranate
Behind your veil.
[4]Your neck is like the tower of David,
Built with rows of stones
On which are hung a thousand shields,
All the round shields of the mighty men.

In verse 1 he told her she was beautiful, *but surely any man can tell a woman she is beautiful,* so he took it a step further. He described her eyes as mesmerizing and beautiful. He said they revealed the gentleness of her spirit.[2] As he lifted up her veil and placed it over her hair, he said her hair was beautiful, shiny, and luxurious. It's about time guys noticed our hair! She probably spent days trying to get her hair to look that good! *Good job, Solomon!* He softly ran his fingers over her lips and complimented her for having beautiful lips and perfect teeth. The "pomegranate" description represented her sweetness, and her neck displayed her strength and dignity.

Solomon was patient and selfless. This is harder for guys because they have a hyperactive sexual imagination and drive, and they are usually *always* ready for sex. He was mature and perceptive enough to know when to move out of verbal foreplay and into physical foreplay. He was sensitive and gentle with his bride. He didn't just take her to the honeymoon suite and rip her clothes off. He didn't move fast, and it seemed like he did everything humanly possible to help his bride relax and feel at ease. Also, notice how creative, romantic, and thoughtful he was. It is *always* easier to communicate with physical touch than it is to use words to describe your feelings and emotions, but again we see how Solomon was a champ: first he used his words, then his hands. He wooed his wife and almost teased her a little because he spent so much time talking to her. He seduced her so slowly that she was probably ready for sex long before he initiated the sexual acts between them.

In verses 1–4, Solomon's compliments started with his bride's hair, then he moved to her face and neck. We will see in verses 5–7 how he moved his eyes down her body and complimented her on every area of her body.

> [5]Your two breasts are like two fawns,
> Twins of a gazelle
> Which feed among the lilies.
> [6]Until the cool of the day
> When the shadows flee away,
> I will go my way to the mountain of myrrh

And to the hill of frankincense.
[7]You are altogether beautiful, my darling,
And there is no blemish in you.

Notice the change between verse 4, "Your neck is like the tower of David, built with rows of stones on which are hung a thousand shields, all the round shields of the mighty men," and verse 5, "Your two breasts are like two fawns, twins of a gazelle which feed among the lilies." In verses 1–4, Solomon complimented his bride's heart and character, as well as her outer beauty. In verse 5, he transitioned into sexual talk and caresses. As he talked about her neck, he must have slowly slipped off her top and he was now looking at her breasts. He described her breasts as the fawns that feed among the lilies, meaning they were beautiful and perfect. In describing her breasts he used the words *two* or *twin* three times in one verse. *Three times!* He was probably close to stuttering at that point. They literally stumped his brain so that all he could say was something like, "You have really, really nice breasts, really." That's funny.

In verses 6 and 7, Solomon was telling his bride how he now wants to enjoy sexual pleasures with her *all night long*. He was being honest and vulnerable with her. The "mountain of myrrh" and the "hill of frankincense" described the woman's breasts. As part of the woman's preparation for her honeymoon, during the days, months, and years preceding the wedding, she wore a bag around her neck that contained a mixture of fragrant spices and oils. This was to ensure that she smelled really, really good for her spouse. This bag hung in between her breasts, which is why Solomon probably called them the "mountain of myrrh" and the "hill of frankincense."[3] He probably was fondling her breasts and absorbing the luscious smell of her.

In verse 7, we can conclude that she was naked with him. As they explored each other's bodies, he said that every last inch of her body was beautiful. As Solomon complimented his bride from her head to her feet, notice what the bride said. Nothing. She didn't say a word! She did not interrupt him. She did not tell him he was wrong, lying, or exaggerating. She received his compliments. Ladies, when your husband gives you compliments, smile and say thank you. Stop trying to convince him that he is wrong or needs glasses. Start believing what he says. It will change your life—and your future sex!

For the men reading this book, let me tell you that wives want to hear how you are attracted to her character and her body *daily*. I am sure men need to hear this daily from their wives too! This practice of finding ways to love and bless your spouse daily will make your marriage fun and exciting. The same is true in sex. Both husbands and wives want to know when their spouse delights in them. Men, don't ever think you can give too many compliments to your wife. Sex and love in a marriage are supposed to encourage both people.

Beginning in verse 8, we see how Solomon invited his bride to make their vows final by uniting in sex.

> [8]Come with me from Lebanon, my bride,
> May you come with me from Lebanon.
> Journey down from the summit of Amana,
> From the summit of Senir and Hermon,
> From the dens of lions,
> From the mountains of leopards.
> [9]You have made my heart beat faster,
> my sister, my bride;
> You have made my heart beat faster
> with a single glance of your eyes,
> With a single strand of your necklace.
> [10]How beautiful is your love, my sister, my bride!
> How much better is your love than wine,
> And the fragrance of your oils
> Than all kinds of spices!

> [11]Your lips, my bride, drip honey;
> Honey and milk are under your tongue,
> And the fragrance of your garments is like
> the fragrance of Lebanon.

Twice in verse 9, Solomon told her, "You have made my heart beat faster." Essentially he was saying that she sexually aroused him and he didn't want to put off sex any longer. By Solomon taking time to slowly arouse his wife, he was also aroused and ready to move out of foreplay and into the actual sex act. In verse 10, the Hebrew word *love* here means "romantic love": they were having sex. Notice the punctuation used here too. He emphasized his words to further emphasize his pleasure. As they made love he told her how wonderful she was and affirmed her. This text is so arousing (and I am only reading about it)! Solomon understood how delicate and sensitive women are and how they are aroused by what they hear. How could sex get any better than this?

Something very interesting happened while they were having sex: Solomon thanked his bride for keeping herself sexually pure.

> [12]A garden locked is my sister, my bride,
> A rock garden locked, a spring sealed up.
> [13]Your shoots are an orchard of pomegranates
> With choice fruits, henna with nard plants,
> [14]Nard and saffron, calamus and cinnamon,
> With all the trees of frankincense,
> Myrrh and aloes, along with all the finest spices.
> [15]You are a garden spring,
> A well of fresh water,
> And streams flowing from Lebanon.

Our culture makes fun of virgins and thinks there is something wrong with you if you are single and aren't having sex; we see the opposite response from Solomon. This may seem like a weird thing to say when you are at the sexual climax of making love, but the fact that she waited for him and saved those sexual moments for him to experience at that very moment was special. Even before she knew him, she waited for him, and that aroused him and made sex all the more intoxicating and romantic. They honored God with their sex life before they married (by not having sexual relations) and now, during sex, they honored God by enjoying sex with each other. Sex in marriage is meant to join the couple, produce offspring, keep the couple from outside sexual temptations, provide mutual plea- sure and fulfillment, and did I mention that sex is supposed to be pleasurable?

Song of Solomon ends chapter 4 with words from his bride. This was the first time she spoke in this chapter and look at what she said. What she said was probably one of the most erotic things a man can hear while having sex:

> [16]Awake, O north wind,
> And come, wind of the south;
> Make my garden breathe out fragrance,
> Let its spices be wafted abroad.
> May my beloved come into his garden
> And eat its choice fruits!

She told him how badly she wanted him sexually, *all of him*. She wanted to be engulfed with his sexual pleasure and be completely one with him. She wanted to please him any way *he* chose. Notice the exclamation point when she said this to her husband. Although in the Hebrew language there is no such thing as an "exclamation point," our English translation carries the emphasis intended in the text. We get the point here. *Wow, that's intense.* That is what it is like to wait until you are married to have sex. Take a minute and breathe

. . . you probably haven't done this in a couple minutes. Relax a little so you can finish reading this chapter!

Sex Reflections

We are not done talking about sex just yet. We can observe a few more things about verses 4:5–16. First, reflect on what this couple said to each other and did for each other. Solomon was the initiator and his wife responded accordingly, but they were *both* vulnerable. They talked about sex during the experience of it. Great sex doesn't just happen, it requires communication, humility, selflessness, and work. Solomon and his bride did these things, which was why they had such intoxicating sex. Solomon wasn't a "natural" at sex or communicating. He coupled his desire for his wife with his effort and gave his wife one of the best gifts a wife can get from her husband—he was a selfless lover.

Never underestimate the power and influence a man has when he leads his bride by being selfless and giving. Solomon's efforts to serve and adore his bride blessed their marriage and sexual relationship. When you get married, it will take time and communication to have fun and intoxicating sex, so be patient with each other as you grow in the learning process together. At first your husband might be so aroused just seeing you naked that he might not be able to contain his excitement, and that's okay. Getting two bodies to move and act as one takes time, but your time will come. I have no doubt that when you save sexual intimacy for your spouse, both you and your husband will be able to relate to the intimacy and enjoyments that this couple shared in the Song of Solomon.

Second, sex is supposed to refresh you and give you life, just like Solomon said in 4:15: "A fountain of gardens, a well of living waters, and streams from Lebanon." Like a bottle of water after a long day of surfing, these two lovers' sexual thirst was quenched. This couple honored each other and indulged in pure, unadulterated sexual pleasures simultaneously. They did nothing immoral, perverse, vulgar, or crude—this is the reward of saving sex for marriage.

Third, notice how the couple did not just experience the touch of sex, but they experienced sex with all five senses. Touch, taste, smell, sight, and hearing are all a part of great sex in marriage. Only when this couple married did they indulge and delight in all of the senses. This kind of satisfaction and vulnerability is available and freeing when both individuals know that the other is committed to the marriage *for life*. Because of their commitment, they felt comfortable and secure enough to be themselves and enjoy each other. In marriage, real sexual intimacy occurs when you aren't afraid to be completely vulnerable, when your sexual relationship is void of alternative motives, and when your sexual relations really are an expression of your commitment to love each other.

Fourth, unlike singles who have sex, during and after sex Solomon's and his wife's pleasure was not interrupted with thoughts like, "Maybe this time he will realize he should commit to me," "I hope we don't get caught," or "I hope I don't get an STI or pregnant." The level of security and love that was experienced by Solomon and his bride cannot be found in casual sex relationships or any type of sexual relationship outside of marriage. Solomon's actions and words made his wife feel secure, loved, and desirable. Verse 5:1 records the first thing he said to her after they had sex:

> I have come to my garden, my sister, my spouse;
> I have gathered my myrrh with my spice;
> I have eaten my honeycomb with my honey;
> I have drunk my wine with my milk. (NKJV)

After descending from the peak of sexual pleasure, this bride was probably both excited and nervous. She was exhilarated by the sexual experience with her husband and wondering what he thought about their experience. *Was it good for him too, or was he just pretending? Is he glad he waited for me? Is he glad he married me? Did he enjoy pleasing me? Was it what he hoped for?* These sensitive issues are important to address. Sexual nourishment requires maturity, sensitivity, love, and the security of marriage to discuss freely.

Solomon showed us the main difference between couples who have sex outside of marriage and couples who wait until they're married. What Solomon said to his bride not only encouraged her and reassured her of his delight in her, but it reminded her of his commitment to her *for life*. The words "I have come" in verse 5:1 show us that he was speaking of something he already did. Line by line he recalled the foreplay, kissing, fondling, and sex as he assured her that he thoroughly enjoyed it all. He repeated phrases that he said earlier so she could see how he loved *everything*, every last thing. He used the word *garden* to show her he delighted in the sex.[4] The words *myrrh* and *spice* affirmed his enjoyment in her breasts.[5] The words *honeycomb* and *honey* referenced the pleasure he found in her lips, every single time she used them to speak or touch his body, and he also used the word *milk* to tell her how he loved kissing her.[6] He concluded his statement with, "I have drunk my wine with my milk"—meaning their passionate sex left him completely satisfied. Literally he was saying, "It doesn't get any better than this."

What I love most about the ending of this sex scene is the underlying theme, which is sacrificial love. From what I've heard about sex, it's quite a workout for the husband and wife. Immediately after the peak of the sexual activity Solomon could have fallen asleep, but instead he chose to affirm his wife again. It's as if they were lying on their bed, bodies intertwined, as he whispered in her ear how much he enjoyed her and how he loved that they had become one. This must have made his bride feel so special. He complimented and encouraged her before, during, and after sex in a sincerely romantic way, and *then* he fell asleep. Just kidding, the text doesn't say that, but it's probably the truth.

In Song of Solomon chapter 7, Solomon's wife was so aroused and encouraged by her husband's words that she went out of her way to give her husband that same pleasure. Great sex in marriage is supposed to give *both* the husband and the wife fulfillment and enjoyment. In these verses we see how this bride felt so loved by her husband that she initiated sex with him.

> ¹⁰I am my beloved's,
> And his desire is toward me.
> ¹¹Come, my beloved,
> Let us go forth to the field;
> Let us lodge in the villages.
> ¹²Let us get up early to the vineyards;
> Let us see if the vine has budded,
> Whether the grape blossoms are open,
> And the pomegranates are in bloom.
> There I will give you my love. (NKJV)

From what I hear, it arouses, excites, and encourages a man when his wife initiates sex. It makes a husband feel wanted and desired by his wife. On Solomon's wedding night, he initiated and asked for sex, but in 7:10–12 we see the roles changed. In verse 10, this bride invites Solomon to have sex with her. Not only did she initiate sex, but she surprised Solomon by suggesting they add a change of scenery to their lovemaking (with the talk of lodging in villages, vineyards, etc). What married man doesn't want his wife to surprise him by spicing up their sex life? These verses are so cool because this couple first took the time to communicate and establish a relational foundation in which they felt secure enough to verbalize their love and desire for each other. They didn't hold back when they communicated their sexual desires for each other. I don't know about you, but this is my kind of honeymoon! This is the type of sexual relationship I am willing to wait for, no matter how long it takes.

Although I am sure sex doesn't always score a perfect ten on the charts, when both partners are honestly, lovingly, and selflessly communicating their likes and dislikes to each other, they have higher satisfaction levels. Even if the sex-o-meter isn't off the charts, the "oneness," or the connection of being so physically close to each other, is priceless.

I am such a sucker for all this stuff. I am the epitome of the romantic type. A few things I love about this couple's relationship in Song of Solomon are the absence of pride, arrogance, and selfishness. This story really drives home the point that great sex and great marriages are for the individuals who are selfless. We don't see Solomon or his bride demanding sex, or ordering the other person around. This couple never once said something bad about the other person. We don't know exactly how old this couple was when they were married, but we know that they didn't have sex with each other until they were married. They probably were excited to make up for lost time, but they did not act in a way that was demanding or self-centered.

Solomon made a habit of blessing his wife before, during, and after sex. His love was giving and selfless. Overall, he was more concerned with making sure his wife was happy than worrying about his own needs. Both individuals expressed their heart's desire and sought to love and satisfy the other person, all the while showing no signs of pride or self-centeredness. Because their focus was not on themselves, they were able to share in mutual satisfaction and sensual pleasure that was untainted, unbridled, and uninhibited.

Obviously no one is perfect. I am sure that this couple had their moments (perhaps many moments). But the fact that they waited to have sex until they were married, and that they took pleasure in their lovemaking once they were married, testifies to the goodness of trusting God's plan for sex.

In marriage, sex is supposed to be the glue that holds the couple together, not the foundation that keeps them standing. As we observe King Solomon and his wife's marriage, we see that they give us three tips on how to have a great marriage: 1) Keep each other sexually pure until marriage; 2) Keep the romance going after the honeymoon; and 3) Make sure marriage gives life and encouragement to each spouse.

Isn't It Romantic?

Married couples who make romancing each other a priority are those who have learned the importance of not taking their spouse for granted. Women want to date a romantic guy *and* be married to one too. Go figure. Wives need romance! Some men think that once they are married they can relax. They don't think it is important to go on dates anymore, but Solomon shows that men should continue to pursue and adore their wife.

Solomon was great at encouraging his wife and being sexual with her *after* their honeymoon. Look at this text from chapter 7. Notice the verbiage that is repeated from before, but also notice his effort to affirm his bride using words and phrases:

> [1]How beautiful are your feet in sandals,
> O prince's daughter!
> The curves of your thighs are like jewels,
> The work of the hands of a skillful workman.
> [2]Your navel is a rounded goblet
> Which lacks no blended beverage.
> Your waist is a heap of wheat
> Set about with lilies.
> [3]Your two breasts are like two fawns,
> Twins of a gazelle.
> [4]Your neck is like an ivory tower,

Your eyes like the pools in Heshbon
By the gate of Bath Rabbim.
Your nose is like the tower of Lebanon
Which looks toward Damascus.
⁵Your head crowns you like Mount Carmel,
And the hair of your head is like purple;
The king is held captive by its tresses.
⁶How fair and how pleasant you are,
O love, with your delights!
⁷This stature of yours is like a palm tree,
And your breasts like its clusters.
⁸I said, "I will go up to the palm tree,
I will take hold of its branches."
Let now your breasts be like clusters of the vine,
The fragrance of your breath like apples,
⁹And the roof of your mouth like the best wine. (NKJV)

He encouraged, affirmed, and enticed her with his words. He could have demonstrated the attitude of "I told you that I loved you when we got married and if it changes I'll let you know," but we see how he found even more ways to express his love for his wife.

In addition to being mutually fulfilled by sex, they had a great understanding of the continual love that sustained them. In chapter 8, the bride said to her husband:

⁶Set me as a seal upon your heart,
As a seal upon your arm;
For love is as strong as death,
Jealousy as cruel as the grave;
Its flames are flames of fire,
A most vehement flame.
⁷Many waters cannot quench love,

> Nor can the floods drown it.
> If a man would give for love
> All the wealth of his house,
> It would be utterly despised. (NKJV)

The phrases "strong as death" and "many waters cannot quench" seem to be the most romantic and honest words I have heard this couple say so far. Experts say that the emotions evoked from having sex in marriage are so intense and so deep that the level of emotional intensity can only be compared to what it is like to see someone die. *That is intense.*

When love is as deep and as committed as what this couple had, they would not let anything or anyone come between them. These words remind me of the wedding vows I have often heard: "To have and to hold, from this day forward, for better, for worse, for richer, for poorer, in sickness or in health, to love and to cherish 'til death do us part." This couple understood the importance of making a lifelong commitment to each other and to God. Every marriage will have good times, bad times; times of change, growth, happiness, and sorrow. But only the couples who are committed to a continual love will finish their journey happy and together. That's the kind of marriage I want!

Unlike the average chick flick or romance novel, love stories don't end when people get married. They simply change their words from "I do" to "I will" as they live the rest of their lives together. From what I have seen and heard, being married to the love of your life is one of the coolest things ever. Which is why in the next chapter I will give you a glimpse of a couple whose lifetime commitment to each other changed my life (both before and after they were married).

God, the Matchmaker

NO ONE WANTS TO BE TRAPPED in an unsatisfying sex life "until death do us part." *Myself included.* You might wonder, "What if I save sex for marriage and the sex is terrible?" But do you see the underlying issue here? The question you really want answered is, "Can I trust God with my relationships and even my sexual satisfaction?" The answer to this important question is a resounding yes!

Don't forget the promises God has given to each of us as believers. Before you can have a great dating or marriage relationship, and definitely before you can have a fabulous sex life, you need to trust God. People trust God to help them with their grades, college choice, and future career, but they are afraid to trust God with their relationships and sex life.

If Christians are asked if they trust God, no doubt they will quickly respond in a robotic tone with a yes. But do we *really*? If we really trusted God with every area of our lives, we would not have sex outside of marriage. If we really trusted God, we wouldn't wonder if sex will be good in marriage, and we wouldn't believe the lie that we are "missing out" by saving sex for marriage. We would trust what His Word says, and we would trust His character. We would remember that when God gives us a boundary, it is simply because of His love for us.

God gives us sexual commands and restrictions to help us have a prosperous, full, and exciting life. But we forget this and we don't trust that He—more than anyone—is looking out for our best interest. So we doubt God, justify our sexual behavior, and refuse to believe that God actually has plans—great plans—for our sex lives. Why is it so hard for us to trust God with our romantic relationships? God knew exactly what He was doing when He commanded us to save sex for marriage. But we forget all of this when we are single, sexually stimulated, and wanting sex *now*!

God Knows What We Desire and What We Need

To some, Christianity appears to be all about rules. They think God is bossy, controlling, and an ardent "joy killer" because He commands us not to have sexual relations outside of marriage. The truth is God is creative and fun. Don't believe me? Just look at Adam's life. As we read the book of Genesis, we stand in awe as we watch God exist on His own and create a universe of things visible and invisible: light, stars, planets, moon, oceans, swimming creatures, land, land creatures, birds, insects, flowers, trees, and plants. Then God decided to make the most complex and complicated creature of all—God created a *man*. Out of all the created objects and beings, God must have wanted a bigger challenge, and boy, did He get it. Men are some of the strangest creatures alive!

After creating Adam, God told him to work. Adam had two job

titles: Head Botanist and Chief Zoologist of every living thing that
God created. *Talk about interesting jobs!* As Adam faithfully labored
in the work God gave him, *God* decided that something was missing.
Adam didn't know anything was missing—the Bible said he lived in
paradise. Genesis 2:18 tells us how relationships began: "Then the
LORD God said, 'It is not good for the man to be alone; I will make
him a helper suitable for him.'" This verse has so many key points.

Did you catch that? *God* saw Adam needed something more.
God knew what Adam needed . . . a woman. Notice what *didn't*
happen here. Adam didn't ask God for a woman. Adam didn't drop
hints or draw pictures of women and leave them out for God to see.
Adam didn't even know what a woman was. Creating Eve was not
Adam's idea, she was God's idea. Next God said, "It is not good for
man to be alone." This shows us that God really does know us. He
cares about us so much and is so connected with our heart, soul,
and mind that He knows what we need before we do. He knows our
desires for today and for our future. He knows how I desire the companionship of a husband, and how hard it gets for me to be single
sometimes. He knows I want to get married and have a family. He
knows I want to be loved and love a man deeply. God knows.

The same way God knows me, God knew Adam. Adam was
doing what he did best as Head Botanist and Chief Zoologist when
God pulled him aside to affirm the work he had done so far. I imagine the conversation to have started like this: "Adam, I am so proud
of you. You have obeyed what I told you to do and I have enjoyed
watching you work. But now I've got a little surprise for you . . ."
Have you ever surprised someone? Sometimes it is so hard for me
to keep a secret, especially if it is an amazing surprise that I know
the person will love! Giving gifts is so much fun when the person is
surprised, grateful, and totally excited about their gift. I can picture
God being overwhelmed with excitement and trying to steady His
voice as He said to Adam, "You have been working really hard. You

should take a short nap, and when you wake up you will be *pleasantly* surprised." This is my rough translation of course, but you get the point. Adam was in for the surprise of his life!

God was the first to say that it was not good for the man to be single, and He was the one who created Eve to be Adam's wife. God meticulously formed Eve from Adam's rib, and in doing so He created her to "suit" Adam. The definition for *suitable* is "worthy of being chosen especially as a spouse; someone who is desirable or worthy."[1] After creating Eve, God didn't make it confusing for Adam to find his bride-to-be. He didn't make Adam jump through hoops or wait. In Genesis 2:22, we read that *God* brought Eve to Adam. Upon seeing the woman, Adam was so proud of her that he gave her the name *Eve*, which in the original Hebrew language means "life giver." In addition to being able to bear children, a wife can give life to her spouse spiritually, physically (e.g., energy and excitement), emotionally, relationally, and mentally. So too the husband gives to his wife. Hebrew names were usually given to describe something that occurred upon birth (and in this case, creation). When Adam first saw Eve, he knew she was created to bring him life.

After introducing Eve to Adam, God didn't waste any time to marry them. Upon marrying them He gave them a few commands: He told them to indulge, enjoy, and be saturated in the pleasures of being naked and having sex with each other. *If I were God, I would have kept my speech short too. Before they sinned, Adam and Eve walked around naked, and honestly, how long can a man and woman stare at each other naked before they start having sex?* Although God probably spoke as fast as an auctioneer does at an auction, the wedding ceremony must have felt like an eternity for both of them. I live in a world where men *wear* their clothes and I sometimes get so turned on I can hardly think straight. I can't imagine how I could be productive if I were surrounded by *naked* men. *Thank you God that men wear clothes now!* Not only did God approve of their being naked, He commanded them to become one as a married couple and to unite sexually.

God provided for Adam simply because He loved him. This is the same God we can trust. This is the God we *need* to trust, especially with our relationships and sexuality. Just as God provided for Adam's needs—before Adam even knew he had a need—so now we can trust that God will provide for our every need. Although His provision may not end up being exactly as we pictured it, God always provides for us.

Greatness in sex and relationships begins with trust. Trusting God with our sexuality is our duty; learning what He commands and allows sexually in a marriage is our pleasure. This may sound foreign to you, but when you have sex with your husband, you are *blessing* God. Weird, huh? Sex in marriage is a gift from God, and when we enjoy the gift, we make God glad. It's similar to the story above with Adam and Eve: God gave Adam and Eve the gift of each other, marriage, intimacy, sex, and all the blessings that come from this type of union.

Very few of us have seen a marriage comprised of two individuals who stayed committed to the promises they made each other on their wedding day, but I have. It wasn't until my mom met my stepdad that I was convinced that men like him really existed. It wasn't until they met that I was able to really trust God with bringing me my future husband . . . but I am getting ahead of myself. Let me start from the beginning.

Can You Really Find True Love on an Airplane?

I don't want to date another man for a long time, she thought as she accidentally slammed the car door of her now ex-boyfriend. She and Matt dated for more than a year, and now their relationship was over. Valorie, my mom, was tired from an emotionally exhausting weekend. With tears and puffy eyes, she stood at the airport ticket counter, where all she heard the lady say was, "We were able to get you on the next flight to Denver." She was usually a vibrant, fun, beautiful thirty-eight-year-old woman, but for now, she couldn't stop crying. She tried to tell herself that the breakup was for the best, but all she could do was cry.

After living in Arizona for a year and a half after her divorce, my mom, my sister, and I moved back to our home state, Colorado. I remember Mom being super busy with work, dating Matt long distance, and making new friends. Reflecting back on it now and knowing how much time and energy dating relationships take, I don't know how she did it.

Surprisingly, I was overly opinionated at a young age and I always told Mom how I felt about guys she dated . . . what else was expected from a thirteen-year-old girl? Here are some conclusions I came to at the ripe old age of thirteen: There are basically four different types of guys in this world. There are "good guys"—the kind who seem nice, are interested in you, someone you are willing to get to know better, but no initial sparks. There are "great guys"—the kind who started off as a good guy, you got to know them better and realized that they were everything you had said you wanted on that list of qualities you want your future husband to have, but there is no chemistry. There are the "wrong guys"—the kind who are just bad for you in every area, but for some reason you are physically attracted to them. And finally, there is "the one"—the guy who you and your entire church have been praying for since before you were born; the one you know you can't live without.

Matt seemed nice and Valorie thought Matt was a "great guy," but for her, he never turned into "the one." After dating for more than a year in the same city and then long distance, their relationship ended when Matt asked Valorie to marry him and she said no. She was scheduled to spend the rest of the weekend in Arizona, but instead she insisted that Matt take her to the airport early in hopes of getting on an earlier flight back to Colorado.

During that same weekend two men by the names of Bill and Mark were scheduled for a red-eye flight from Colorado to Phoenix, where Bill was scheduled to speak at an Athletes International Ministry conference. Bill frequently received speaking requests because of his career, so this was not an unusual trip at all, at least not until they arrived in Las Vegas. The saying, "What happens in Vegas, stays in Vegas" is never true and it wasn't true in this case either. Mark was sad about something so he asked Bill to pray for him. "Bill, I am lonely. I really want a family: a wife, kids, and a dog." Mark was forty-one and tired of being single. To Mark's surprise, Bill insisted that they pray about this immediately. In the middle of the Las Vegas Airport, with slot machines all around them, they both got on their knees and prayed for God to bring Mark a wife and family.

Mark and Bill had a tiring weekend in Arizona and anxiously anticipated getting some much-needed sleep on the plane ride back to Colorado. When they checked in at the gate, the flight attendant looked a little confused as she told the men, "I don't understand what happened, but your seats have been separated." Both men were so tired from the long weekend that they weren't too bothered by the fact that their seats were separated. They just wanted to get home. When they approached the waiting area near their gate, Mark noticed a pretty woman near the gate, but he didn't think anything of it.

Valorie was able to subdue her tears and focus her remaining energy on preparing to sleep on the airplane. She had hoped to have the row to herself, so when a kind-looking man sat next to her and began reading his Bible, she rolled her eyes. After her breakup with Matt, she was trying to distance herself from men, not be trapped next to one for a two-hour plane ride. Whether it was the bright reading light that the man next to her was using or her post-breakup anxiety, she soon realized that she was not going to be able to sleep on this flight. Although she couldn't sleep, she definitely didn't want to talk either, even though the man next to her was reading his Bible. It was around this time that she realized the flight attendant had already passed her row and she wanted coffee. When she finally flagged down a flight attendant for a cup of coffee, the man next to her insisted that she take his. *Great,* she thought, *now I really have to talk to this guy . . . that was so nice of him.* So she put her agenda aside and decided, *I will never see this man again, so what the heck, let's talk.*

Well, as it turned out, she knew this man, or at least she knew *of* him. His name was Coach Bill McCartney, affectionately known as "Coach Mac." He not only was a Christian, but was the founder of Promise Keepers, an organization that encourages guys to be godly men. That and he was the head coach of college football's 1990 national champions, the Colorado Buffaloes. Although Coach Mac's face had been on the cover of every sports magazine, newspaper, and cable network, in her defense, Valorie was not exactly a sports fanatic. Actually, she wasn't really a sports fan at all, so although she had heard him speak at a conference earlier that year, she didn't recognize him.

As she told Coach Mac about her faith and her recent breakup, he was so expressively excited that he almost spat on her when he said, "Maybe you're the one I was praying for." Well, of course Valorie had no idea that Coach Mac was remembering how he prayed for Mark a day earlier in the Las Vegas airport. She didn't even know Mac had a friend on the plane. Suddenly Coach Mac's face changed and with his intense but sincere tone he said, "I wish you would have sat by Mark." It seemed as if Mac had been a host for a dating show as he began telling her all of the amazing qualities and characteristics about Mark and why she would benefit by going out with him. Coach Mac was obviously scheming when he said, "Why don't we exchange business cards and when the plane lands I'll point Mark out to you. If you think he's cute I'll give him your card and tell him to call you. Mark is about six foot four inches, has brown hair, blue eyes, and looks like Tom Selleck."

When the plane landed Mac pointed to Mark, Valorie thought he was handsome, and she told Mac to have Mark call her. For some reason guys think that they should wait a couple of days before calling a girl. I have never really understood this. But when a week went by and instead of receiving a call from Mark, she received a postcard from Mac saying, "Mark is going to call you soon," she got frustrated. For one, she couldn't stop thinking about Mark; day and night he was on her mind and she had never even met the guy. For six weeks this continued until her friends were sick of hearing about it and she was sure that God was sick of her praying about it. She decided that there was only one thing left for her to do, call him. She decided that she would call him, but after that she wouldn't do anything else to initiate contact with him. If he called her back, great, if not, well then she could at least try to move on.

You are probably wondering why Mark didn't call Valorie. Good question. For starters, he was dating someone else at the time and ending the relationship was harder for him than he had anticipated. Mark wanted to maintain his character and integrity through the breakup. As if Mark didn't have enough things on his mind, every day without missing a beat Coach Mac hounded him about Valorie, "Did you call her yet?" Day after day this continued. When Mark finally ended his dating relationship and was ready to make the elusive phone call, he realized he had another problem: he couldn't find Valorie's business card. He planned to look for it at home and if all else failed he would ask Coach Mac for her contact information.

But before he had a chance to look for the lost business card, that day at work when he answered his phone he heard a woman say, "Hi, I'm Valorie; does my name sound familiar?" When Mark told

Valorie his story of how he lost her number, she thought something that almost every woman is bound to think in this type of circumstance: *What a liar. If you can't be honest enough to tell me you aren't interested in me then forget it . . . you don't have to make up stories for why you never called.* Despite her initial thoughts about him, she agreed to go to lunch with him the following week.

It was at that lunch that something special happened between them. When they were together the time seemed to pass so quickly. They went on several more dates and after about a month of dating consistently, they both knew they were in love. Although they almost broke up on their one-year anniversary when, after they finished their fabulous dinner at the best restaurant in town, Mark looked deeply into Valorie's eyes and slid a little red box across the table. What she thought was the most exciting moment in their relationship quickly turned into the saddest moment. What she expected to find in the little velvet box was an engagement ring. What she found was a brooch. A stinking brooch! She couldn't *not* thank him for such a lovely brooch simply because she was hoping for an engagement ring. But she was mad, and sad, and worried, and before Mark knew what happened, they were in an argument. Really, she was just afraid that Mark wasn't ready to commit to having a wife and two teenage drama queens. Mark, like most men, took longer than Valorie wanted to wait, but when he finally asked for her hand in marriage, it was a happy day for everyone. And when they married, it was the best day of our lives, aside from the hideous dress my mom made me wear. Without a doubt, Mark was the best thing that had ever happened to us (aside from our relationships with God, of course). He was the best man I have ever known.

It is funny how God answered Mark and Mac's prayer that day in the Las Vegas airport. They prayed on a Saturday and the very next day my mom sat next to Coach Mac on the airplane, and the rest is history. Mark and Mom got married when I was fourteen, on July 3, 1993. It is an amazing thing when two people pledge their whole lives to each other in front of God and everyone. It is an even more glorious thing to see them keep their promises. Mark was handsome, wise, funny, kind, and a guy that everyone seemed to love. There wasn't a place in the world that we went where he wasn't greeted with a smile and a hug by someone who knew him. He was a great husband and dad. Even during all of our teenage drama, Mark never once raised his voice . . . I still don't know how he was able to do that.

On July 3, 1993, as I stood there looking at Mark, I knew that one day I wanted to marry a man just like him. Lucky for us, we serve a big God and I know that it's possible. Every time I talked with Mark about guys and my desire to get married, he would stop and we would pray. It didn't matter if I was on my way to the gym, the grocery store, work, or a date, Mark always reminded me of two things: you can trust God to take care of your desire for marriage, and you never know how God will introduce you to your future spouse. Every time I talked to Mark about the guys who asked me out or ones who didn't know I existed, regardless of the story, as long as they were Christian men he always reminded me, "You never know how God will bring you and your husband together." And it's true, you never know.

Calling All Cities

Join the No Sex in the City Movement and Be the First to Make a Change in Your City

VISIT www.LindseyIsham.com FOR MORE INFORMATION

As if I haven't been transparent enough in this book, I want to take the next few pages to tell you my heart, and let you know why I took the time to write this book especially for you.

When people say that "casual sex" is no big deal, they are really saying that *they* are no big deal . . . and they are so wrong. You are a big deal. You have a God who loves you intimately and thinks that you are so precious. You have gifts, beauty, and talents that no one else has. You are a gift from God! This is the complete and honest truth.

In the past, you may have been around people who didn't treat you as the special person you are. You may have been in situations with guys when they did something with you that you hadn't done before. You weren't sure that you wanted them to continue (even if you did enjoy the feeling), but you felt too paralyzed to do something about it.

Sex and sexual acts may have been things that you gave away, or maybe they were taken from you. Regardless of your past, you are still such a gem. You, *yes* you, deserve nothing but the best. Really—nothing but the very best.

Today I ask you to look deep inside your heart. As you have read this book, certain guys, certain words, and certain events have come into your mind. You want to believe what I have written, but for some reason you still think that you have made too many mistakes, you have been with too many guys, or you don't think you deserve abstinence again.

Every day people try to convince you that it isn't possible to wait to have sex until marriage, sex isn't worth waiting for, or that you aren't worth waiting for. Please don't listen to them. Listen to God. Listen to the same God who knew you and loved you before you were a thought in your parents' mind. Listen to the God who knows your every thought, word, and action, and *still* desires to have a close relationship with you. Listen to God, the Father who loves you more than anyone could ever love you. He wants the best for you; He loves you and says that you are worth it!

In Proverbs 31:10–31, Solomon describes a virtuous wife. In verse 12, he says this about a virtuous wife: "She brings him good, not harm, all the days of her life" (NLT). In Hebrew, the original language of this verse, the word *good* meant "pleasing" in the widest sense: to better, cheer, be good, make good, please, do well. This type of woman will bring good things to her husband. She is fine, glad, gracious, joyful, kind, likable, loving, merry, and pleasant. She is precious, prosperous, sweet, fair, and looks out for herself and others.[1]

We are inspired to be like this woman, but the definition isn't limited to married women. Notice the second part of the verse reads "all the days of her life." This means in our past, today, and in our future. The choices and actions you make today will have a huge impact on your future husband, family, and generations to come. If you desire for your future husband to say to you one day, "You have brought me good, and not harm, all the days of your life," then I challenge you to make a few choices that will forever change your life and the lives of others in your city.

Choice #1

The first decision is the most important decision you will ever make in your life—that is to choose Christ to be your Lord and Savior. If it weren't for His gracious sacrifice on the cross, giving up His own sinless life to save us from our sinful lives, we would not have a hope for the future. Without God, we cannot receive or give love or forgiveness. If we are honest with ourselves, we can admit that we are not perfect. Our lack of perfection makes us, by definition, sinners. Because we are sinners, there is nothing we could ever do to earn our way to heaven. In order to spend eternity with God in heaven, you must admit to Him that you believe you are a sinful person and that you also believe that the only way to heaven is through accepting the fact that Jesus died for your sins, paid the price for your sins when He was killed on a cross, and when He rose from the dead on the third day He proved that nothing can keep Him from being who He really is—God. Tell God you believe in Him and ask Him to be the Lord of your life. Then ask Him for forgiveness of your sins. This is the first and biggest step to living for God.

Some of you may think it's too late for you to have a relationship with God. And many of you think that you have already done too much sexually, but it is never too late to come clean with God.

King David, the man who committed adultery with a married woman and then killed her husband, prayed the prayer of forgiveness that you see below in Psalm 51 (NLT). His prayer was heartfelt and genuine, and God loved him for that. God forgave David of his sins, and He will forgive you of your sins too. Maybe his prayer could help you express your sorrow for your past sins (especially sexual sins). Pray this prayer:

> Have mercy on me, O God,
> because of your unfailing love.
> Because of your great compassion,
> blot out the stain of my sins.
> Wash me clean from my guilt.
> Purify me from my sin.
> For I recognize my rebellion;
> it haunts me day and night.
> Against you, and you alone, have I sinned;
> I have done what is evil in your sight.
> You will be proved right in what you say,
> and your judgment against me is just.
> For I was born a sinner—
> yes, from the moment my mother conceived me.
> But you desire honesty from the womb,
> teaching me wisdom even there.
>
> Purify me from my sins, and I will be clean;
> wash me, and I will be whiter than snow.
> Oh, give me back my joy again;
> you have broken me—
> now let me rejoice.
> Don't keep looking at my sins.
> Remove the stain of my guilt.
> Create in me a clean heart, O God.
> Renew a loyal spirit within me.
> Do not banish me from your presence,
> and don't take your Holy Spirit from me.

Restore to me the joy of your salvation,
and make me willing to obey you.
Then I will teach your ways to rebels,
and they will return to you.
Forgive me for shedding blood, O God who saves;
then I will joyfully sing of your forgiveness.
Unseal my lips, O Lord,
that my mouth may praise you.

You do not desire a sacrifice, or I would offer one.
You do not want a burnt offering.
The sacrifice you desire is a broken spirit.
You will not reject a broken and repentant heart, O God.
Look with favor on Zion and help her;
rebuild the walls of Jerusalem.
Then you will be pleased with sacrifices offered in the
right spirit—
with burnt offerings and whole burnt offerings.
Then bulls will again be sacrificed on your altar.

After you have confessed that you are a sinner, start growing your relationship with Jesus. He loves you so much!

Choice #2

Abstinence is refraining from all sexual activity. Sexual activity is not limited to sex, but also includes other actions intended to result in sexual arousal or gratification. Sex includes penile-vaginal, anal, and oral sex. Other actions intended to result in sexual arousal or gratification include, but are not limited to, masturbation, mutual masturbation, fondling, the use of sex toys, and the viewing of pornography. Abstinence is the healthiest behavior for unmarried individuals.

Secondary virginity is a return to abstinence following a sexual debut. A commitment to secondary virginity is often made with the goal of remaining abstinent until marriage. Increasing numbers of teens and young adults are making this decision not only to reduce their considerable risk for sexually transmitted infections and non-marital pregnancies, but also because they want to do what is pleasing to God.

Today, make the commitment, not just to wait until marriage to have sex, but also to wait for all sexual acts. Let's be honest, you don't have to have sex to be sexually stimulated. Instead of asking how far you can go with a guy sexually, ask yourself, "How far will I go to bless my future husband? How much of myself will I save for him?" Don't give yourself away to Counterfeits anymore. Save yourself, all of yourself, for your husband. Even if you have already done or have imagined doing every sexual act possible, you can experience the joy, freedom, and love of Christ by changing your lifestyle and sexual decisions.

Abstinence and secondary virginity are personal decisions. You can't be pressured or guilted into either of them. The decision has to be a desire of your heart for it to be real for you and to enable you to live an abstinent lifestyle. Today is the day to change the statistics that say 88 percent of teens who take an abstinence pledge break it.[2] By making this promise to God and your future husband, and by keeping your word, you will change those statistics.

Throughout this book I have given you the reasons to wait and tips on how to wait. Now it is up to you to live out the convictions you have made today. They will require courage, delayed gratification, self-discipline, and discernment. You can't make this commitment on your own; it will take the power of God and the help of close friends and mentors as well. Love yourself enough to know that you are worth waiting for; both you and your future husband will be so grateful that you waited for him!

The No Sex
in the City Plan

Create a Plan

- Give your life to God and ask Him for wisdom and guidance.
  Learn what the Bible says about sex.
- Use the buddy system. Don't believe the lie that you can succeed
  at abstinence by walking the purity road alone. Prayerfully choose
  another friend (of the same sex) to ask you the tough questions
  and help keep you on the road of excellence. Choose a friend
  who also wants to live an abstinent lifestyle. It will be such an
  encouragement to you to have an accountability partner and friend
  who you can turn to when others tease you and try to pressure you.
- Establish your sexual boundaries before you are in a relationship.
  (See chapter 7 for a reminder of some of my boundaries and advice.)
- Be realistic with yourself. You know your strengths and

weaknesses—set yourself up to succeed, not to fall back into the same old sexual patterns.

- Get a mentor. No matter one's age or status, we are never too old, nor too wise, to have someone else speaking loving-kindness and truth into our lives.
- Share your plan with your parents and ask them for advice and to help you make wise decisions in this area.

Create Life Goals

Remember, abstinence is not forever; it's only until marriage. There are other important things to think about before and after marriage. The decisions you make today will impact your future family!

- Who do you want to be as a woman, daughter, sister, friend, student, athlete, employee, etc.?
- What do you feel God is calling you to do with the talents He's given you?
- What do you want your future family to look like?

Memorize Scripture

Memorize Scripture to encourage you and help you through the difficult times you will face once you make the promise to be abstinent.

> O naive ones, understand prudence;
> And, O fools, understand wisdom.
> —Proverbs 8:5

> But among you there must not be even a hint of sexual immorality, or of any kind of impurity, or of greed, because these are improper for God's holy people.
> —Ephesians 5:3

Put to death, therefore, whatever belongs to your
earthly nature: sexual immorality, impurity, lust, evil
desires and greed, which is idolatry.

—Colossians 3:5

It is God's will that you should be sanctified: that
you should avoid sexual immorality; that you should
abstain from fornication.

—1 Thessalonians 4:3

Marriage should be honored by all, and the marriage
bed kept pure, for God will judge the adulterer and all
the sexually immoral.

—Hebrews 13:4

If we claim to have fellowship with him yet walk in the
darkness, we lie and do not live by the truth.

—1 John 1:6

Notes

CHAPTER 1: YOU'RE A WHAT?

1. Jason Fields and Lynne M. Casper, *America's Families and Living Arrangements*, issued June 2001, Current Population Reports, P20-537, U.S. Census Bureau, pp. 9–11, http://www.census.gov/prod/2001pubs/ p20-537.pdf.
2. Table MS-2, "Estimated Median Age at First Marriage, by Sex: 1890 to Present," U.S. Census Bureau. Internet release date: Sept. 15, 2004; http://www.2010census.biz/population/socdemo/hh-fam/tabMS-2.pdf.
3. Sharon A. Hersh, *Mom, Sex Is No Big Deal!* (Colorado Springs: Shaw, 2006), 22.

CHAPTER 2: GIRLS AREN'T SUPPOSED TO BE HORNY, ARE THEY?

1. 2 Timothy 2:22.
2. Romans 3:10; Matthew 26:41 and Mark 14:38; and Jeremiah 17:9.
3. 1 Corinthians 7:9.
4. Isaiah 55:8.
5. Genesis 39:9.
6. Genesis 37–50 tells the story of Joseph.

CHAPTER 3: YOU'RE MISSING OUT!

1. "You Tell Us," 2004 readership survey, *Young and Modern* (August 2004): 78.

2. Romans 12:1 supports this idea.

3. More than a few sources show similar conclusions on this topic. See, for example, Pam Stenzel's DVD, *Sex Has a Price Tag: A Compelling Look at Sex in the New Millennium* (Grand Rapids: Rooftop Productions for Stenzel-Drummond & Assoc., 2000); the 2004 ABC News *Primetime* live poll by Cheryl Arnedt, Gary Langer, and Dalia Sussman, "The American Sex Survey: A Peek Beneath the Sheets," http://abcnews.go.com/Primetime/News/Story?id=156921&page=1; and David Gudgel's book, *Before You Live Together* (Ventura, CA: Regal, 2003).

4. Arnedt, Langer, and Sussman, "The American Sex Survey."

5. Gudgel, *Before You Live Together,* 46.

6. According to the National Institute of Allergy and Infectious Diseases, "Sexually transmitted infections (STIs), once called venereal diseases, are among the most common infections in the United States today. More than twenty STIs have now been identified, and the Centers for Disease Control and Prevention estimate they affect more than 19 million men and women in this country each year. The annual medical costs of STIs in the United States are estimated to be up to $14 billion." ("Sexually Transmitted Infections," http://www3.niaid.nih.gov/healthscience/healthtopics/sti/default .htm.)

7. Stuart Berman, Willard Cates Jr., and Hillard Weinstock, "Sexually Transmitted Diseases Among American Youth: Incidence and Prevalence Estimates, 2000," *Perspectives on Sexual and Reproductive Health* 36, no. 1 (January/February 2004): 6–10, www.agi-usa.org/ pubs/journals/3600604.html.

8. Ibid.

9. Several sources cited the inaccuracy of condom claims. "Condoms have a poor record for prevention of pregnancy, with failure rates of up to 13% or more per year" (E. F. Jones and J. D. Forrest, "Contraceptive Failure in the United States: Revised Estimates," *Family Planning*

Perspectives 21, no. 3 [May/June 1989]). "A meta-analysis of condom effectiveness from in vivo studies by Dr. Susan Weller suggests a 31% failure rate in preventing HIV transmission" (Weller, "A Meta-Analysis of Condom Effectiveness in Reducing Sexually Transmitted HIV," *Social Science and Medicine* 36, no. 12 [1993]). Trojan-brand condom packaging reads, "If used *properly*, latex condoms will *help reduce* the *risk* of transmission of HIV infection (AIDS) and many other sexually transmitted diseases. Also highly effective against pregnancy" (italics added for emphasis). Notice that the word *protection* is not used in this label, but the word *risk* is.

10. Associated Press, "Condom Label Changes Spark Debate," CBS News (April 2, 2004), http://www.cbsnews.com/stories/2004/04/02/health/main610112.shtml.

11. See Centers for Disease Control and Prevention, "Genital HPV Infection—CDC Fact Sheet," http://www.cdc.gov/std/HPV/STDFact-HPV.htm#prevent; and Nicole Gottlieb, "A Primer on HPV," *Benchmarks* 24, no. 4 (April 24, 2002), available from the National Cancer Institute, http://www.cancer.gov/newscenter/benchmarks-vol2-issue4/page2.

12. American Pregnancy Association, http://www.americanpregnancy.org/main/statistics.html.

13. Guttmacher Institute, "U.S. Teenage Pregnancy Statistics National and State Trends and Trends by Race and Ethicity," updated September 2006, http://www.guttmacher.org/pubs/2006/09/12/USTPstats.pdf.

14. Guttmacher Institute, "Facts on American Teens' Sexual and Reproductive Health," updated September 2006, http://www.guttmacher.org/pubs/fb_ATSRH.html.

CHAPTER 4: NUDE BEACHES AND MY CURIOSITY

1. "Virginity and the First Time," *SexSmarts* (October 2003), publication 3368, http://www.kff.org/entpartnerships/upload/Virginity-and-the-First-Time-Summary-of-Findings.pdf. (SexSmarts is an information

partnership between the Kaiser Family Foundation and *Seventeen* magazine.)

2. "Heart to Heart," *Seventeen* (September 2003): 128.

3. 2002 National Longitudinal Study of Adolescent Health, cited in Robert W. Blum et al., "Mothers' Influence on Adolescents' Sexual Debut," *Journal of Adolescent Health* 31, no. 3 (2002).

4. Tommy Nelson, *Song of Solomon*, sermon on CDs. Based on his book *The Book of Romance: What Solomon Says About Love, Sex, and Intimacy* (Nashville: Thomas Nelson, 2007).

CHAPTER 5: GIRLS GONE CRAZY?

1. All of these verses require a plan: Proverbs 16:1, 3–4, 9, 33; 18:22; 1 Timothy 2:9–11; 3:21–22. See also these verses for similar ideas: Genesis 2:18, 21–25; Proverbs 5:15–19; 12:4; 19:14; 31:10–31; 8:35; 24:27; Matthew 22:4, 8; 24:44; 25:10; Mark 14:15; John 2:1–11; 1 Corinthians 13: 4–8; 1 Peter 3:1–6, 7–12.

2. Fields and Casper, *America's Families and Living Arrangements*, 9–11.

3. Neil Clark Warren, *Finding the Love of Your Life* (Wheaton, IL: Tyndale, 1992), 13.

4. 1 Corinthians 7:1, 7. See also Matthew 19:4–11 and 1 Corinthians 7 for more specific instructions.

CHAPTER 6: BRINGIN' SEXY BACK

1. A 2006 Barna study found that 44 percent of men nationwide compared with 50 percent of women have attended a church service, not including a special event such as a wedding or a funeral, in the past seven days (http://www.barna.org/FlexPage.aspx?Page=Topic&TopicID=10).

2. U.S. Census Bureau, estimation as of February 14, 2008, http://www.census.gov/population/www/popclockus.html.

3. The statistics and analysis come from national surveys conducted by Barna Research in 2006, http://www.barna.org/FlexPage.aspx?Page=Topic&TopicID=10.

4. Bella DePaulo and E. Kay Trimberger, "Single Women: Sociologists for Women in Society Fact Sheet, Winter 2008," http://74.125.95.132/search?q=cache:gwIOGPsQUDkJ:www.socwomen.org/wint08_fs.pdf+single+adult+men+united+states+2007&hl=en&ct=clnk&cd=7&gl=us.

5. See John Piper, *What's the Difference?* (Wheaton, IL: Crossway, 1990).

6. John Witte Jr,. *From Sacrament to Contract: Marriage, Religion, and Law in the Western Tradition* (Louisville: Westminster John Knox Press, 1997), 49. See also the works of Martin Luther ("The Estate of Marriage") and John Calvin (*Institutes*; *Commentary on the Epistle of Paul the Apostle to the Corinthians*; *Commentary on a Harmony of the Evangelists*, vols. 16/22). Calvin writes that the "choice to marry is not put in our own hands, as if we were to deliberate on the matter" and that those who willingly and knowingly refuse or delay marriage should be viewed as "carefree" and "foolish." Dr. Albert Mohler thinks today's church has forgotten that marriage is not just a social activity. He states,

> According to the Bible, marriage is not primarily about our self-esteem and personal fulfillment, nor is it just one lifestyle option among others. The Bible is clear in presenting a picture of marriage that . . . [t]he man and woman are made for each other and the institution of marriage is given to humanity as both opportunity and obligation. . . . The Bible assumes that marriage is normative for human beings. The responsibilities, duties, and joys of marriage are presented as matters of spiritual significance. From a Christian perspective, marriage must never be seen as a mere human invention—an option for those who choose such a high level of commitment—for it is an arena in which

God's glory is displayed in the right ordering of the
man and the woman, and their glad reception of all
that marriage means, gives, and requires. Clearly,
something has gone badly wrong in our understanding
of marriage. This is not only reflected in much of
the conversation and literature about marriage as
found in the secular world, but in many Christian
circles as well. The undermining of marriage—or at
least its reduction to something less than the biblical
concept—is also evident in the way many Christians
marry, and in the way others fail to marry.

("Looking Back at 'The Mystery of Marriage,' Part 1," August 19, 2004,
http://www.crosswalk.com/news/weblogs/mohler/?adae=8/19/2004.)
7. Austin Scaggs, "Justin Timberlake Revs Up His Sex Machine" *Rolling
Stone* 1009 (September 21, 2006), www.rollingstone.com/news/
story/11514699/cover_story_justin_timberlake_revs_up_his_sex_
machine/7.

CHAPTER 7: EVALUATING HIS SPERM COUNT
1. 1 Corinthians 15:33.
2. Jeremy Vohwinkle, "Marriage: Tying the Financial Knot," http://
financialplan.about.com/cs/personalfinance/a/Marriage.htm; and "Why
Money Is the Leading Cause of Divorce," *Jet* (November 18, 1996).

CHAPTER 8: MY TWO CENTS ABOUT DATING
1. John 13:34.
2. Song of Solomon 2:7; 3:5; 8:4.
3. James 1:14–15.
4. Gudgel, *Before You Live Together*, 39–49.
5. 1 Corinthians 10:32.
6. Ephesians 5:33.

CHAPTER 10: SEX, PLEASE

1. In the Jewish culture during King Solomon's day, after a man proposed to a woman (and she accepted), he left her to go build their new home. On the night before he left his bride-to-be, they ate a meal together at the engagement party. The promise of marriage was binding and to "seal the deal," the bride-to-be drank wine from the "shared cup," which represented the marriage covenant. The bridegroom would say to his fiancée, "Although I will not drink wine again until I see you, drink this wine in remembrance of me. Every time you drink wine, remember that I am coming back for you." (The couple would drink wine together next at their wedding ceremony.)

   After drinking wine from the shared cup, the bridegroom gave gifts to his fiancée and her family and promised to return for her. Then he would go to his father's house to build a new house for his bride, which was usually attached to or close by his father's house. The fiancée didn't know when her groom would return and neither did he. He could only come back to get her when his father said that all the preparations were adequate. Because she didn't know how long it would take, each day she woke up knowing that today could be her last day living with her family. ("A Fresh Look at the Jewish Wedding," [Phoenix: Mayim Hayim Ministries, 1998], http://www .mayimhayim.org/JewishWedding.htm)

   Solomon's fiancée, because she was marrying the king, went through beautification treatments and purification rites for a year before she saw her future husband. She went through washings to symbolize that she was being washed from the past and ready to start a new life with her husband. She was bathed, soaked, and rubbed with scents and oils.

2. "The eye is the lamp of the body. If your eyes are good, your whole body will be full of light. But if your eyes are bad, your whole body will be full of darkness. If then the light within you is darkness, how great is that darkness!" (Matthew 6:22–23).

3. Early D. Radmacher, ed., *Nelson's New King James Study Bible* (Nashville: Thomas Nelson, 1997), 1100.

4. See Song of Solomon 4:12, 15.

5. See Song of Solomon 4:6, 13–14.

6. See Song of Solomon 4:11.

CHAPTER 11: GOD, THE MATCHMAKER

1. "Suitable," Dictionary.com, WordNet® 3.0. Princeton University, http://dictionary.reference.com/browse/suitable.

CONCLUSION: CALLING ALL CITIES

1. James Strong, *The New Strong's Exhaustive Concordance of the Bible* (Nashville: Thomas Nelson, 1990), 2895–96.

2. Hannah Bruckner and Peter Bearman, "After the Promise: The STD Consequences of Adolescent Virginity Pledges," *Journal of Adolescent Health* 36 (2005): 275.